Notting Hill Gate 5A

Workbook

Für Klasse 9 an Gesamtschulen
und anderen integrierenden Schulformen
Differenzierende Ausgabe
Advanced course

Diesterweg

Notting Hill Gate 5A

Workbook für Klasse 9 an Gesamtschulen und anderen integrierenden Schulformen
Differenzierende Ausgabe
Advanced course

Herausgegeben von:
Dr. phil. h. c. Christoph Edelhoff, StD a. D.,
Vorsitzender THE ENGLISH ACADEMY

Erarbeitet von Michael Biermann, Otfried Börner, Hannelore Debus, Phil Mothershaw-Rogalla, Sabina Piatzer, Ingrid Preedy und Kathleen Unterspann, sowie Ingrid Gebhard und Pat Jüngst

Fachliche Beratung: Natalie Beer, Lieselotte Bohnsack, Melanie Dahm, Arno Esser, Rolf-Olaf Geisler, Susanne Hooß-Biehl, Stephanie Mayer, Angelika Pohlmann, Cornelia Scherer, Dr. Annegret Staufer, Noah Tauche und Michael Tetzlaff

Beratung Portfolio und QAR: Sanja Wagner

Inhalt

Theme 1	3
Theme 2	17
Theme 3	33
Exam practice	44
Exam practice Lösungen	54
Theme 4	59
Theme 5	73
Theme 6	84
Survival English	98
Survival English Lösungen	112
Language in Focus	116
QAR	127
Portfolio-Fragebögen (Einleger)	

Weitere Zusatzmaterialien zum Schülerbuch
(978-3-425-10605-1)

- Audio-CDs für Schüler 978-3-425-10665-6
- Workbook mit Audio-CDs 978-3-425-10665-0

© 2011 Bildungshaus Schulbuchverlage
Westermann Schroedel Diesterweg
Schöningh Winklers GmbH, Braunschweig
www.diesterweg.de

Das Werk und seine Teile sind urheberrechtlich geschützt. Jede Nutzung in anderen als den gesetzlich zugelassenen Fällen bedarf der vorherigen schriftlichen Einwilligung des Verlages.
Hinweis zu § 52 a UrhG: Weder das Werk noch seine Teile dürfen ohne eine solche Einwilligung gescannt und in ein Netzwerk eingestellt werden. Dies gilt auch für Intranets von Schulen und sonstigen Bildungseinrichtungen.
Auf verschiedenen Seiten dieses Buches befinden sich Verweise (Links) auf Internet-Adressen.
Haftungshinweis: Trotz sorgfältiger inhaltlicher Kontrolle wird die Haftung für die Inhalte der externen Seiten ausgeschlossen. Für den Inhalt dieser externen Seiten sind ausschließlich deren Betreiber verantwortlich. Sollten Sie bei dem angegebenen Inhalt des Anbieters dieser Seite auf kostenpflichtige, illegale oder anstößige Inhalte treffen, so bedauern wir dies ausdrücklich und bitten Sie, uns umgehend per E-Mail davon in Kenntnis zu setzen, damit beim Nachdruck der Verweis gelöscht werden kann.

Druck A[1] / Jahr 2011
Alle Drucke der Serie A sind im Unterricht parallel verwendbar.

Redaktion: Barbara Drauschke, Jutta Eckardt-Scheurig, Amy Koerner, Laura Lanik, Dr. Katja Nandorf, Verena Nungesser und Sabina Piatzer
Herstellung: Harald Thumser, Frankfurt
Illustrationen: Ulf Marckwort, Kassel
Umschlaggestaltung: Blum Design & Kommunikation, Hamburg
Satz: fotosatz griesheim GmbH, Griesheim
Druck und Bindung: pva Druck und Mediendienstleistungen GmbH, Landau

ISBN 978-3-425-**10615**-1

Notting Hill Gate 5A
Portfolio-Fragebögen

Name: _____

Klasse: _____

Diesterweg®

Liebe Schülerin, lieber Schüler,

Portfolio-Fragebögen kennst du schon aus den letzten vier Schuljahren. Sie können dir dabei helfen, einen Überblick darüber zu bekommen, was du schon beherrschst und woran du noch arbeiten solltest. Du füllst die Fragebögen jedes Mal aus, wenn ihr ein Theme im Textbook (TB) und Workbook (WB) komplett abgeschlossen habt.

Hier zur Erinnerung nochmals die Anleitung:

Sieh dir z. B. die Sätze zum Hören an. Lies die Sätze und überlege, wie gut du das kannst, was dort beschrieben ist. Hinter jedem Satz steht, wo du nachschlagen kannst, wenn du nicht genau weißt, was gemeint ist.

Es kann auch sein, dass ihr im Unterricht nicht alle Übungen gemacht habt. Dann kannst du den betreffenden Satz überspringen.

Hinter jedem Satz kannst du ein Symbol eintragen, das zeigt, wie gut du etwas schon kannst:

Wenn du meinst, dass du etwas schon gut kannst, dann mache in der grünen Spalte ein Häkchen ✔.

Dir fällt etwas noch schwer? Dann male einen Kreis O in die gelbe Spalte. Lies dann die angegebene Stelle im Textbook (TB) oder Workbook (WB) nach. Hier kannst du die Fertigkeit noch einmal üben.

Wenn du etwas noch nicht kannst, dann mache einen Strich — in der roten Spalte. Sieh dir die passenden Stellen im TB und WB noch einmal ganz genau an. Am besten blätterst du dann zurück zu den vorigen Fragebögen und schaust nach, wie du deine Kenntnisse dort eingeschätzt hast.
Du kannst dir dann noch einmal die passenden Stellen im TB und im WB anschauen.

Auf der letzten Seite findest du einen Fragebogen, in dem du am Ende der Klasse 9 selbst beurteilen kannst, wie du deine Fertigkeiten (oder Kompetenzen) einschätzt.

Und jetzt: Viel Spaß!

Was ich nach *Theme 1* schon kann

	Ich kann ...	Material Aufgabe	Seite	✔ Das kann ich gut.	O Das fällt mir noch schwer.	— Das kann ich noch nicht.
Hören, Hör-Seh-Verstehen	auf Einzelinformationen achten, um meine Ergebnisse zu korrigieren.	WB A5b, B7b	6, 13			
	die wesentlichen Aussagen in einem Film verstehen.	TB A9 WB A11	14 9			
	gezielt Informationen/Schlüsselwörter verstehen und notieren, wenn es um Themen geht, die ich kenne.	TB A8, A11c WB A6	14, 15 7			
Lesen	ein Gedicht verstehen.	TB B2	16			
	Schlüsselbegriffe im Text finden.	WB B2a	10			
	Meinung und Begründung in einem persönlichen Bericht zu einem bestimmten Thema verstehen.	TB B3, B5a	17, 18			
	Informationen aus mehreren Texten zusammentragen.	WB B6c	12			
QAR	gezielt im Text nach Antworten suchen und beschreiben, wie ich sie gefunden habe.	WB B8	13			
Sprechen monologisch	meine Meinung begründen.	TB A3 ☀, B 3b	11 17			
Sprechen dialogisch	über die Ergebnisse einer Umfrage sprechen.	TB A1	10			
	über verschiedene Extremsportarten sprechen.	TB A2, A3	11			
	verschiedene Extremsportarten miteinander vergleichen.	WB A3	4			
	meine Meinung begründen und an Beispielen erläutern.	TB A3 ☀, B5	11, 18			
Schreiben	darüber schreiben, was ich im Hochseilgarten vielleicht tun würde.	WB A8d ★	8			
	den Inhalt eines Textes zusammenfassen.	TB B5b WB B4	18 11			
	meine Meinung zu einem Thema aufschreiben.	TB A8c	14			
Kombination von Fertigkeiten	Informationen zu einem Thema sammeln und auf Englisch einen kurzen Vortrag halten.	TB A10, A13, B10 WB A2	14, 15, 19 3			
	eine Umfrage durchführen und darüber berichten.	TB B1e	17			
Sprachmittlung	meinem Partner Fragen zu einem deutschen Text auf Englisch beantworten, wenn ich das Thema kenne.	TB A7, B5 WB B9	13, 18 15			
	einen englischen Text auf Deutsch zusammenfassen.	TB B5d	18			
Lern- und Arbeitstechniken	in einem Wörterbuch Wörter nachschlagen.	WB A8	8			
	Informationen aus Tabellen wiedergeben.	WB B1	10			
	ein Wortnetz erstellen.	WB A1c	3			
Wortschatz	„weder noch" auf Englisch richtig anwenden.	TB B9, P7 WB B4	19, 21 11			
	Bedeutung von unbekannten Wörtern aus dem Kontext klären.	WB A4	4			
Grammatik	sagen, wie lange ich etwas schon mache.	TB A4 WB A5	12 6			
	Modalverben situationsgerecht anwenden.	TB A6, P5 WB A6b	12, 21 7			
	Passivformen des Verbs erkennen und bilden.	TB B6, P6	18, 21			
	zwischen *for* und *since* unterscheiden.	TB A5 WB A5	12 6	✔		

Was ich nach *Theme 2* schon kann

	Ich kann ...	Material Aufgabe	Seite	✔ Das kann ich gut.	O Das fällt mir noch schwer.	— Das kann ich noch nicht.
Hören, Hör-Seh-Verstehen	auf Einzelinformationen achten, um meine Ergebnisse zu korrigieren.	WB A10	23			
	gezielt Informationen/Schlüsselwörter aus Beiträgen verstehen und notieren, wenn es um Themen geht, die ich kenne.	TB A4, B5	27, 33			
		WB A7, B13	21, 31			
Lesen	in Sachtexten zu einem bekannten Thema Informationen finden.	TB A2c, A3, A7	25, 26, 28			
	Stellenanzeigen verstehen.	TB A2, B2	25, 30			
	Informationen aus mehreren Quellen zusammentragen.	TB B1c	29			
		WB B6c	26			
	einem Text gezielt Informationen entnehmen.	TB B4b	32			
QAR	gezielt nach Antworten im Text suchen und beschreiben, wie ich sie gefunden habe.	WB B12	29			
Sprechen monologisch	den Inhalt eines Textes wiedergeben.	TB B3b ☼	31			
	eine Stellungnahme abgeben.	TB B5e	33			
Sprechen dialogisch	über Erfahrungen im Praktikum sprechen.	TB A1	24			
	Rollenspiele vortragen.	TB B3c ☼	31			
		WB B9	28			
Schreiben	meinen Lebenslauf nach einem Modelltext schreiben.	TB A3c, B7	26, 33			
	eine Bewerbung schreiben.	TB B7	33			
	eine Stellenanzeige schreiben.	TB A6	27			
Kombination von Fertigkeiten	Informationen zu einem Thema sammeln und auf Englisch ein kurzes Rollenspiel vortragen	TB A6, B7	27 33			
	Informationen zu einem Thema sammeln, um einen Bericht zu schreiben.	TB A6, B7 Nr. 4	27 33			
	Informationen zu einem Thema sammeln und auf Englisch einen kurzen Vortrag halten.	WB A6 Nr. 1-2	21			
Sprachmittlung	Informationen in einem englischen Text sammeln und darüber auf Deutsch berichten	WB A3	18			
Lern- und Arbeitstechniken	Texte verbessern.	WB A6 Nr. 3-4	21			
	wichtige Textabschnitte markieren.	WB B6	26			
Wortschatz	Wortschatz zum Thema *soft skills* sammeln.	WB A4, B1	19, 24			
	wichtige Ausdrücke in einem Modelltext finden.	TB A2b, c, A3e ☼	25 26			
Grammatik	Zeitangaben in der indirekten Rede richtig anwenden.	WB A10	23			
	Ratschläge formulieren (*If*-Sätze Typ I).	TB P5	35			
		WB B2, B8	24, 27			
	berichten, was jemand gemacht hat (indirekte Rede).	TB A5, P2, P6, WB A9	27, 34 35, 22			
	das *past perfect* auf Ereignisse anwenden, die vor einem anderen passiert sind.	WB A8	22			
	berichten, was gefragt wurde.	TB B5d, P7, WB B9b	33, 35 28			

Was ich nach *Theme 3* schon kann

	Ich kann …	✔ Das kann ich gut.	O Das fällt mir noch schwer.	— Das kann ich noch nicht.
Hören, Hör-Seh-Verstehen	Tonaufnahmen die wichtigsten Informationen entnehmen.			
	die wichtigsten Informationen verstehen, wenn ich Filme, Dokumentationen oder Videoclips ansehe.			
Lesen	in Büchern, Zeitungen, Zeitschriften oder im Internet gezielt Informationen zu meinem Projektthema finden.			
	fremde Texte verstehen, wenn ich dabei ein Wörterbuch benutze.			
	wichtige Informationen von unwichtigen unterscheiden, wenn ich Material zu meinem Projektthema sichte.			
Sprechen monologisch	einen kurzen Vortrag mit den wichtigsten Punkten zu meinem Projektthema halten.			
	Einzelheiten meines Themas verständlich erläutern.			
	anschauliche Beispiele geben.			
	lebendig vortragen.			
	weitgehend frei mithilfe weniger Stichpunkte vortragen.			
	auf Fragen zu meinem Vortrag passende Antworten geben.			
	anderen in sehr höflicher Form Rückmeldung zu ihrer Präsentation geben, d. h. ihnen sagen, was ich gut fand und was sie vielleicht beim nächsten Mal verbessern könnten.			
Sprechen dialogisch	mit meiner Gruppe über die Inhalte und die Planung unseres Projekts sprechen.			
	während der Projektarbeit über praktische Dinge sprechen, z. B. Vorschläge für die Gestaltung machen, jemanden um Rat fragen oder andere um Materialien bitten.			
	spontan eine passende Antwort geben, wenn mich andere bei der Projektarbeit ansprechen.			
	in Gesprächen meine Meinung formulieren und begründen.			
Schreiben	kurze Informationstexte schreiben, z. B. für ein Poster, eine Collage oder eine Broschüre.			
	längere Texte schreiben, z. B. einen Artikel, einen Bericht, ein Künstlerporträt oder eine Geschichte.			
	Texte schreiben, in denen ich meine Meinung formuliere und begründe, z. B. ein Statement oder einen Kommentar.			
Kombination von Fertigkeiten	Informationen beim Lesen sortieren und dann für mein Projektthema nutzen.			
	Texte mithilfe von Informationen schreiben, die ich vorher gesammelt habe.			
	die Arbeiten der anderen Gruppenmitglieder beurteilen und ihnen Tipps geben.			
Sprachmittlung	Informationen, die ich auf Deutsch gelesen habe, sinngemäß auf Englisch wiedergeben.			
Wortschatz	Projektvokabular erarbeiten und sinnvoll sortieren.			
	das Projektvokabular verwenden.			
	typische Redewendungen für Präsentationen in einem Vortrag verwenden.			

Meine Projekterfahrungen

Was wir gemacht haben: _____

Thema unseres Projekts: _____

Mitglieder meiner Projektgruppe: _____

Das haben wir präsentiert: _____

_____

Mein Beitrag zu unserem Projekt: _____

_____

Was mir besonders an unserem Projekt gefallen hat:

_____

_____

_____

Was ich bei unserem Projekt gelernt habe:

_____

_____

_____

Was ich gut gemacht habe:

_____

_____

_____

Was mir schwer fiel:

_____

_____

_____

Worauf ich bei Projekten in Zukunft achten möchte:

_____

_____

_____

Was ich nach *Theme 4* schon kann

Ich kann …	Material Aufgabe	Seite	✔ Das kann ich gut.	O Das fällt mir noch schwer.	— Das kann ich noch nicht.
Hören, Hör-Seh-Verstehen					
Sätze und Phrasen verstehen die ich brauche, wenn ich im Hotel ein Zimmer buche.	WB B9	71			
während des Hörens Notizen machen.	TB A4	60			
auf Einzelinformationen achten, um meine Ergebnisse zu korrigieren.	TB P7b	69			
	WBA5, A8	61, 63			
Einzelheiten aus Beiträgen verstehen, wenn es um Dinge geht, die ich kenne.	WB A2, A7	60, 63			
Geräusche/Soundeffekte nutzen, um den Inhalt besser zu verstehen.	TB A1	54			
den Inhalt eines Films verstehen, wenn ich schon etwas über das Thema weiß.	TB B2 c, e	62			
	WB B1	66			
Lesen					
in Sachtexten zu einem bekannten Thema Informationen finden.	People & Places	58, 65			
	TB A3, B5 WB A1	59			
Wertungen in einer Filmkritik verstehen.	TB B1	62			
Informationen aus mehreren Quellen verbinden.	WB A4	61			
den Inhalt eines Liedtextes verstehen.	TB B3	63			
QAR					
gezielt Lesestrategien anwenden, um Fragen zu beantworten und	WB B4	68			
genau beschreiben, wie ich sie gefunden habe.	WB B4	68			
Sprechen monologisch					
über das, was ich gerade erfahren habe, sprechen.	TB A2, B3e	55, 63			
darüber reden, was ich auf einem Foto sehe.	TB A1	54			
den Inhalt einer Grafik beschreiben.	WB A10	64			
Sprechen dialogisch					
mit dem Partner einen Dialog an der Hotelrezeption vorbereiten und vorspielen.	WB B9c	71			
Schreiben					
aufschreiben, was ich gut an Deutschland finde.	TB B8	67			
	WB A2c	60			
meine Meinung zu einem Thema aufschreiben.	TB B1	62			
Kombination von Fertigkeiten					
Informationen zu einem Thema sammeln und auf Englisch einen kurzen Vortrag halten.	TB A3d, A6.1, B6 b, B9	59, 61, 67			
	WB A9, B 11	64, 71			
Sprachmittlung					
über die Informationen aus englischen Texten auf Deutsch reden.	TB A3e, B5b	59, 65			
	WB A11	65			
Lern- und Arbeitstechniken					
Notizen zu wichtigen Informationen aus einem Text/Film erstellen.	TB A3b	59			
	WB B1	66			
statistische Angaben auswerten.	WB A10	64			
einen Zeitstrahl mit Ereignissen erstellen.	TB A3c	59			
Annahmen machen, was in einem Film/Buch passieren wird / Schlussfolgerungen äußern.	TB B3a	63			
Wortschatz					
Zahlen, Datum, Uhrzeit, Prozente und Geldsummen auf Englisch sagen.	TB A5, P2	61, 68			
einige australische Ausdrücke verstehen.	WB A8	63			
nach Regeln neue Wörter ableiten.	WB B5, D3	69, 72			
passende Verben zu Nomen finden *(collocations)*.	WB D3	72			
Grammatik					
Sätze im Passiv bilden.	TB P5, P3	61, 68			
ing-Form richtig anwenden *(likes/dislikes)*.	TB P5	69			
Fragen formulieren.	TB P6	69			
	WB A2, A7b, B8a	60, 63			

Was ich nach *Theme 5* schon kann

	Ich kann ...	Material Aufgabe	Seite	✔ Das kann ich gut.	O Das fällt mir noch schwer.	— Das kann ich noch nicht.
Hören	Einzelheiten aus Beiträgen verstehen, wenn es um Dinge geht, die ich kenne.	TB B2	78			
	auf Einzelinformationen achten, um meine Ergebnisse zu korrigieren.	TB P2b, P3b, P6b WB A3	82, 83 74			
	kurze Beiträge zum Thema Nutzung von Internet verstehen.	TB P2b, WB B2	72 79			
	Argumente für und gegen etwas aufschreiben, wenn es um ein Thema geht, das ich kenne.	TB A2d	73			
	in einem Gespräch verstehen, was zum Thema Internet geäußert wird und von wem.	TB B2 WB A3	78 74			
Lesen	Regeln für die Internetnutzung verstehen und beurteilen, welche auf mich zutreffen.	TB A4	74			
	Texte zu einem bekannten Thema verstehen.	TB A3, B3	73, 79			
QAR	gezielt nach Antworten im Text suchen und beschreiben, wie ich sie gefunden habe.	WB B1	79			
Sprechen monologisch	darüber sprechen, wie ich das Internet nutze.	TB A1	72			
	eine Meinung begründen.	TB A8	77			
	beschreiben, was in einem Bild dargestellt ist.	TB B7	81			
Sprechen dialogisch	mit dem Partner einen Dialog nach einer Vorlage spielen.	TB P2	82			
	einen Dialog für ein Streitgespräch vorbereiten und mit dem Partner vorspielen.	TB A7a	75			
	nach Rollenkarten ein Gespräch führen.	WB B3	80			
	in einer Diskussion/Debatte zum Thema Online-Kommunikation teilnehmen.	TB A7 WB A10	75 77			
Schreiben	über Vorteile und Nachteile der *school of the air* schreiben.	TB B3c	79			
	eigene Erfahrungen zur Arbeit mit dem Computer erläutern.	WB A2	73			
	Vorschläge und Tipps aufschreiben.	TB P6	83			
Kombination von Fertigkeiten	Informationen zu einem Thema sammeln und auf Englisch einen kurzen Vortrag halten.	TB A9, B2, B8 WB B5	77, 78, 81 81			
Sprach-mittlung	Informationen zum Schutz beim Internetsurfen auf Deutsch und Englisch für ein Poster zusammenstellen.	TB A6 ☼	75			
	den Inhalt eines Buches, das ich auf Deutsch gelesen habe, sinngemäß auf Englisch wiedergeben.	WB A9	76			
	auf Deutsch erklären, was in einem Gespräch auf Englisch gesagt wird.	WB B7	82			
Lern- und Arbeits-techniken	ein Wortnetz zum Thema Internet erstellen.	WB A1	73			
	in einem Text passende Wörter für Rätselfragen finden.	WB A11	77			
Wortsschatz	neue Wörter mit Vorsilben bilden.	WB A6	75			
Grammatik	Annahmen/Bedingungen formulieren (*if*-Sätze Typ II).	WB B4	80			
	berichten, was jemand gemacht hat (indirekte Rede).	TB A2c	73			
	den *imperative* benutzen.	TB A6	75			
	conditional clauses 2 benutzen.	TB B6	80			

Was ich nach *Theme 6* schon kann

	Ich kann …	✔ Das kann ich gut.	O Das fällt mir noch schwer.	— Das kann ich noch nicht.
Hören, Hör-Seh-Verstehen	Tonaufnahmen die wichtigsten Informationen entnehmen.			
	die wichtigsten Informationen verstehen, wenn ich Filme, Dokumentationen oder Videoclips ansehe.			
Lesen	in Büchern, Zeitungen, Zeitschriften oder im Internet gezielt Informationen zu meinem Projektthema finden.			
	fremde Texte verstehen, wenn ich dabei ein Wörterbuch benutze.			
	wichtige Informationen von unwichtigen unterscheiden, wenn ich Material zu meinem Projektthema sichte.			
Sprechen monologisch	einen kurzen Vortrag mit den wichtigsten Punkten zu meinem Projektthema halten.			
	Einzelheiten meines Themas verständlich erläutern.			
	anschauliche Beispiele geben.			
	lebendig vortragen.			
	weitgehend frei mithilfe weniger Stichpunkte vortragen.			
	auf Fragen zu meinem Vortrag passende Antworten geben.			
	anderen in sehr höflicher Form Rückmeldung zu ihrer Präsentation geben, d. h. ihnen sagen, was ich gut fand und was sie vielleicht beim nächsten Mal verbessern könnten.			
Sprechen dialogisch	mit meiner Gruppe über die Inhalte und die Planung unseres Projekts sprechen.			
	während der Projektarbeit über praktische Dinge sprechen, z. B. Vorschläge für die Gestaltung machen, jemanden um Rat fragen oder andere um Materialien bitten.			
	spontan eine passende Antwort geben, wenn mich andere bei der Projektarbeit ansprechen.			
	in Gesprächen meine Meinung formulieren und begründen.			
Schreiben	kurze Informationstexte schreiben, z. B. für ein Poster, eine Collage oder eine Broschüre.			
	längere Texte schreiben, z. B. einen Artikel, einen Bericht, ein Künstlerporträt oder eine Geschichte.			
	Texte schreiben, in denen ich meine Meinung formuliere und begründe, z. B. ein Statement oder einen Kommentar.			
Kombination von Fertigkeiten	Informationen beim Lesen sortieren und dann für mein Projektthema nutzen.			
	Texte mithilfe von Informationen schreiben, die ich vorher gesammelt habe.			
	die Arbeiten der anderen Gruppenmitglieder beurteilen und ihnen Tipps geben.			
Sprachmittlung	Informationen, die ich auf Deutsch gelesen habe, sinngemäß auf Englisch wiedergeben.			
Wortschatz	Projektvokabular erarbeiten und sinnvoll sortieren.			
	das Projektvokabular verwenden.			
	typische Redewendungen für Präsentationen in einem Vortrag verwenden.			

Meine Projekterfahrungen

Was wir gemacht haben: _____

Thema unseres Projekts: _____

Mitglieder meiner Projektgruppe: _____

Das haben wir präsentiert: _____

_____

Mein Beitrag zu unserem Projekt: _____

_____

Was mir besonders an unserem Projekt gefallen hat:

_____

_____

_____

Was ich bei unserem Projekt gelernt habe:

_____

_____

_____

Was ich gut gemacht habe:

_____

_____

_____

Was mir schwer fiel:

_____

_____

_____

Worauf ich bei Projekten in Zukunft achten möchte:

_____

_____

_____

So schätze ich meine Fertigkeiten / Kompetenzen in Englisch am Ende der 9. Klasse ein

(Blättere vorher gründlich durch dein Portfolioheft):

✔✔ sehr gut   ✔ gut   O muss ich verbessern

Kompetenz	✔✔	✔	O	Das will ich verbessern:	Das werde ich dafür tun:	Ziel erreicht Datum:	KOMMENTAR
Hörverstehen							
Leseverstehen							
Gespräche führen							
Kurzvortrag							
Schreiben							
Dolmetschen							
Wortschatz							
Aussprache							
Flüssig reden							
Grammatik							
Rechtschreibung							

Ich bearbeite am liebsten Aufgaben zu (Stufe von 1–2–3 bis 4, 1 bedeutet an erster Stelle)

Hörverstehen				
Leseverstehen				
Rollenspiel				
Kurzvortrag				
Text schreiben				
Dolmetschen				
Kleine Projekte				
Wortschatz				
Grammatik				
Aussprache				
(Lektüre)				

Meine Lieblingsthema in diesem Jahr war:

Ich lerne Englisch am besten wenn _____

_____

_____

_____

www.diesterweg.de

Diesterweg®

Meet the challenge **1**

A1 ○ Adventures

a) What comes to your mind when you think of adventures? Make notes. You can use a dictionary.

_____
_____
_____
_____
_____
_____
_____

b) Compare your ideas with a partner's and add further ideas to your notes above.

c) In a group, make a word web about adventures. Then present it to the class.

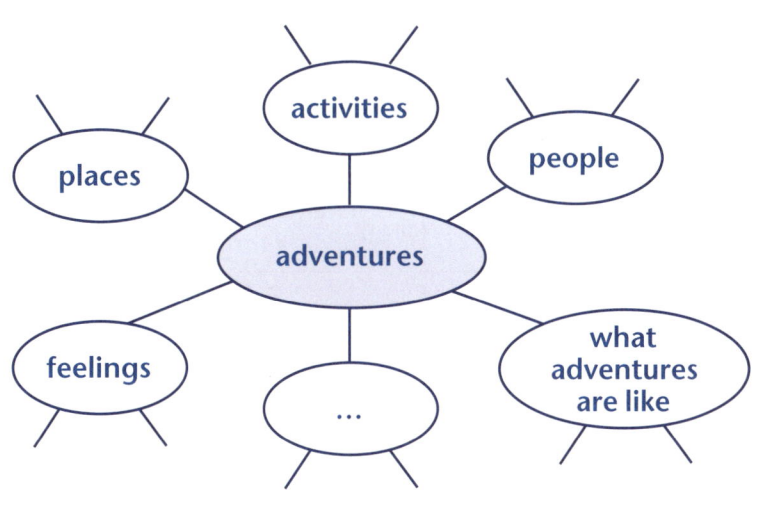

word web:
- activities
- people
- what adventures are like
- ...
- feelings
- places
- **adventures** (center)

portfolio
I can work with words

※ Write a definition of "adventure".

<u>An adventure is</u> _____

portfolio
I can write

A2 ○ Choose

Have you ever done anything adventurous or exciting? Make notes. Think of:

- what you did
- when and where you did it
- who you did it with
- why you did it
- how you did it
- how you felt before, during and after it

1. Use your notes to prepare a three-minute talk. First practise it silently. Then give your talk to a partner or to the class.

2. Use your notes to write a text. Read it out to a partner or to the class.

3. Use good photos and your notes to write a photo story about your adventure.

how to …
talk, write, present

portfolio
I can combine skills

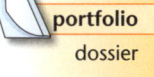

portfolio
dossier

1 Meet the challenge

A3 ● More exciting, more dangerous …

a) Fill in your answers.

1. How exciting do you think these sports are? Number them from 1 to 3.
   (1 = the most exciting   2 = exciting   3 = the least exciting)

   ☐ kitesurfing   ☐ whitewater rafting   ☐ parkour

2. In your opinion, how dangerous are these extreme sports? Number them from 1 to 3.
   (1 = the most dangerous   2 = dangerous   3 = the least dangerous)

   ☐ paragliding   ☐ abseiling   ☐ bouldering

3. Which sport would be interesting to you? Number these sports from 1 to 3.
   (1 = the most interesting   2 = interesting   3 = the least interesting)

   ☐ ice hockey   ☐ ice-skating   ☐ ice dancing

b) Talk about your answers with a partner.

> I think that … is the most / least dangerous of the three sports.

> I think that … is more exciting than …

> I agree.

> I don't think so. I would say …

Watch the videoclip about free skiing on the DVD. Make a new questionnaire like the one above for your partner. Your partner has to fill in his / her answers. You can use some adjectives from the box. Then report some of your partner's anwers to the class.

> challenging • boring • difficult • thrilling • stupid • crazy • …

A4 ○ Harmless or bad for the environment?

a) Read the article from a website and mark new words.

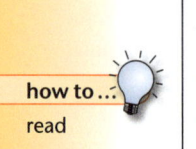

www.url.co.uk

When you go hiking, running or swimming in the sea you can enjoy nature, and as long as you don't leave any rubbish behind, these sports do not have any bad effects on the environment. But it is not always that easy to say whether a sport is harmless or bad for the environment. Basketball, for example, when played as a neighbourhood game, can be nearly as eco-friendly as taking a walk. Yet the famous basketball teams have to fly to hundreds of competitions every year which uses a lot of fuel. The same is true for football. You need nothing but some friends, a ball, and a sunny afternoon to play it – unless you are one of the hundreds of thousands of professionals. Then you'll need buses, cars, and airplanes for both the teams and the large number of travelling fans.

Like basketball and football, some extreme sports also have a bad eco-balance just because people have to be transported to certain places before they can practise the sports. For example, skydiving itself is not harmful to nature, but a plane has to take you up into the air, so a lot of fuel is needed for every jump. During a skydiving competition, planes may have to refuel more than once.

Other extreme sports are even worse because practising them damages the environment.

Meet the challenge **1**

Car races are one example. Although some car companies use new technologies and alternative fuel now, there is really nothing green about the sport. In some races drivers speed around a racetrack again and again for 500 miles, and the events attract large crowds of people who usually drive to the places themselves.

b) Write down new words from the text and use one of the three different ways to find out what they mean. Note down how you found out.

New words	1 The word is similar to the following German word:	2 I could guess from the context¹ that the word means …	3 I used a dictionary and found this translation:

portfolio
I can work with words

¹ context – *Zusammenhang*

c) Look at the text again. What new facts do you learn from it? Mark those facts. Then talk to a partner.

I didn't know that …

I think the most interesting fact is that …

It surprises me that …

d) ★ Write about another sport that can either be harmless or bad for the environment.

☀ Write a last paragraph for the article.

portfolio
I can write

wordbank
sports

_____
_____
_____
_____
_____
_____

5

1 Meet the challenge

A5 • A worried mother

a) Norman's mother has gone on a rafting holiday for a week. One night she calls to find out how Norman and his dad are doing. Use the present perfect progressive and fill in "for" or "since".

Mrs Potts: Well, Norman, I hope you two _____ (do) alright _____ I left.

Norman: Oh sure, Mum. Dad and I _____ (have) a great time. We _____ (eat) nothing but pizza and chips _____ the last few days and we _____ (watch) a lot of great programmes on TV. Oh yes, and we _____ (play) some really exciting computer games, too.

Mrs Potts: What? Where's Dad?

Norman: He's still in bed. In fact he _____ (sleep) _____ eighteen hours now. He _____ (not go) to the office _____ Monday. His boss _____ (call) again and again _____ yesterday morning, but Dad just doesn't feel like answering the phone.

Mrs Potts: What? I'm going to pack my suitcase this very minute and I'll be home by midnight.

Norman: Relax, Mum, just kidding. Dad _____ (go) to work as usual, but he came home early today and _____ (paint) the living room all afternoon.

Mrs Potts: Oh really? How nice of him. I _____ (plan) to do that _____ ages.

Norman: Right, and of course I _____ (help) him _____ I came back from school. Anyway, what about you? How is your holiday?

Mrs Potts: Oh, it's fantastic. The sun _____ (shine) _____ I got here, so I _____ (go) whitewater rafting _____ the last three days. I really _____ (enjoy) myself so far.

Norman: That's great, Mum. I'm happy for you.

Mrs Potts: OK, Norman, please say hello to Dad and look after yourselves. I'll phone again tomorrow. Big hugs, bye.

Norman: Take care, Mum. Bye.

b) Listen to the CD and check the dialogue.

c) Work with a partner. The next day Norman's grandmother calls and wants to find out what he and his dad have been doing. Make notes for a dialogue. Use ideas from the dialogue above and add some new ideas. Act out the dialogue.

Tip: You can often use short forms after "I" and "we".

Meet the challenge **1**

A6 ● Important rules for extreme sports

a) Listen to a radio interview with two experts on extreme sports. What do they say about young people's mistakes and about things that are important or necessary? Take notes.

Mistakes young people make when practising extreme sports

What is important / necessary while doing extreme sports?

b) Use your notes and the words from the box to write eight tips for young people who want to do extreme sports.

> must • have to • should • shouldn't • mustn't

_____
_____
_____
_____
_____
_____
_____
_____

A7 ○ A quiz on sports rules

With a partner, write down six quiz questions about what you must or should think of in order to be safe and successful when doing sports. Write each question on a slip of paper[1] and write the answer on the back. Look at your notes from A6 above and also at A6 in your textbook again.

What equipment must you wear for street BMXing?

What do you have to do when you have an injury?

When should you avoid playing a sport?

Why should you always warm up first?

Now play a quiz game. Work with another pair and ask each other your questions. You get one point for each correct answer. The team with the most points wins. If you would like to play again, then swap[2] your slips of paper with another pair's and form a new group of four.

[1] slip of paper – *Papierstreifen*; [2] swap – *tauschen*

1 Meet the challenge

A8 ○ Having fun at tree2tree

Look at the tree2tree web page from A7 in your textbook again.

a) Find the German words for these English words:

carabiners – _____
extreme speed – _____
high ropes course – _____
rope slide – _____
hell's canyon – _____

b) Use a dictionary to find the English translations for these words:

Areal – _____
Ängste – _____
Spannung – _____
Spinnennetz – _____
Risiken – _____

c) Now use the words from a) and b) to complete the statements.

1. Tree2tree is a _____ which covers an _____ of 20,000 square metres in a park in Dortmund.
2. You can use a rope that throws you into a _____ with _____ .
3. There is also a 100 metre long _____ above the _____ .
4. It is very important to inform yourself about all the _____ before you start using the elements.
5. You must always fasten the _____ the way it is shown in the security instructions.
6. When you go climbing at tree2tree you can learn to get over your _____ and you can also have a lot of fun and _____ .

d) ★ If you could spend a day at tree2tree, what would you do there? Write about your ideas in your exercise book.

☼ Work with a partner. Design a flyer in English for tree2tree.

A9 ● Sound check

a) Mark the stress in these words. The stress in the first word has been done for you.

- extr**e**me
- adrenaline
- backcountry
- underneath
- conditions
- unpredictable
- avalanche
- whitewater
- rapids
- commands
- skydiving
- helicopter
- instructor
- parachute
- experience

b) Listen to the radio show from A8 in your textbook again and check your stresses.

c) Read out the words. Work with a partner and take turns.

A10 ● Describing Alain Robert

a) Look at A11 in your textbook again. Then close the book and complete the sentences.

1. Alain Robert's _____ is French. 2. His _____ is 7 August 1962. 3. His _____ is "The French Spiderman". 4. He is a climber by _____ . 5. He climbs up high _____ and hangs _____ from their tops. 6. Often there are pro-environment and pro-animal _____ on them.

Look at A11 in your textbook again. Then explain these words.

nationality: _____
nickname: _____
occupation: _____
banner: _____
message: _____

b) Find adjectives and phrases to describe Alain Robert and his campaigns.

what he looks like: _____
_____

his character: _____
_____

his campaigns: _____
_____

A11 ○ What happened in Moscow?

a) Watch the interview with Alain Robert from A13 in your textbook again and look at the three photos. What do they show? Take notes while watching. Then write captions[1] for the photos.

b) Write a short newspaper article about Alain Robert's campaign in Moscow. Use your notes from a) and your answers from A13 in your textbook, too.

[1] caption – *Bildunterschrift*

1

Meet the challenge

B1 ⭕ Meat statistics

a) Look at this survey. Write about the most interesting facts. Use these phrases:

The amount of ... has increased.   Americans have eaten more and more .../less ... every year.
At first ... but since ...   The total amount of ...

Amount of meat eaten in the USA (pounds per person)							
year	chicken	turkey[1]	veal[2]	lamb[3]	beef[4]	pork[5]	total
1955	21	4	9	4	56	62	156
1965	33	6	4	3	70	52	169
1975	39	7	3	2	85	43	178
1985	52	9	2	1	77	51	194
1995	69	14	1	1	65	51	202
2005	86	17	1	1	65	50	219

[1] turkey – *Truthahn;* [2] veal – *Kalbfleisch;* [3] lamb – *Lammfleisch;* [4] beef – *Rindfleisch;* [5] pork – *Schweinefleisch*

_____
_____
_____
_____
_____
_____
_____
_____

how to ...
work with statistics

portfolio
I can learn English

b) Work with a partner. Use the survey from a) to make a diagram.

- Decide which figures you want to present. You can use all the figures or just some of them, e.g. only one or two types of meat.
- Decide if you want to design a bar chart or a pie chart.
- Present your chart on a big sheet of paper.
- Hang up all your charts in the classroom and talk about them.

B2 ● Jamila's blog

portfolio
I can read, talk

a) Read B3 in your textbook again. Then choose exactly twelve keywords from the box and underline them.

traffic jam	motorway	transporter	hens	saddest animals
wire fence	bloody beaks	broken wings	missing feathers	eyes
help	awful	service area	salad	real food
growing girl	chicken nuggets	meat	PETA	message

b) Read B3 once again. Then close your textbook and try to tell the story using the keywords you have underlined. Do this silently. If you have problems, look at the text again and underline some different keywords. Don't underline more than twelve!

c) Work with a partner. Tell him or her Jamila's story using your keywords. Take turns.

Meet the challenge **1**

B3 Two cartoons

a) Work with a partner. Describe one cartoon each.

b) Find good titles for the cartoons.

c) Do you think the cartoons are funny? Say why or why not.

☀ Compare the cartoons. What do the cartoonists want to say about vegetarians?

"I've never thought of it as a moral statement; I've just always been a vegetarian."

"No you can't be a vegetarian, son. It just isn't very lion."

B4 Preparing your summary

a) Skim through B5 in your textbook again. Find headings for the three paragraphs and write them down.

	heading	keywords
paragraph 1		
paragraph 2		
paragraph 3		

how to …
read

portfolio
I can read

b) Now read each paragraph carefully and write down three to five keywords from each.

c) Complete the sentences.

The article "Cruelty to Animals: Mechanized Madness" is about _____

_____

Its main message is _____

_____

d) Compare your notes and sentences with a partner's.

e) Now write a brief summary of the article in your exercise book.

how to …
write a summary

portfolio
I can write

1 Meet the challenge

B5 ● A word grid

Look at B5 in your textbook again and find words that match these descriptions.

portfolio
I can work with words

Tip
You can also use the words list on pages 167/168 in your textbook.

1. An area near farm buildings.
2. The space between two places.
3. A situation or an event that you see.
4. A place where animals are killed.
5. Something you can do is … for you.
6. When you … air moves in and out of your body.
7. The power and skill you need to do something.
8. Very dirty.
9. Buses, undergrounds, trains and planes … people from one place to another.
10. Extremely unfriendly actions that hurt people or animals.
11. Stupid, dangerous or crazy actions.
12. Food production is a type of … .
13. If you work hard, you need a lot of … .
14. To become bigger and bigger.

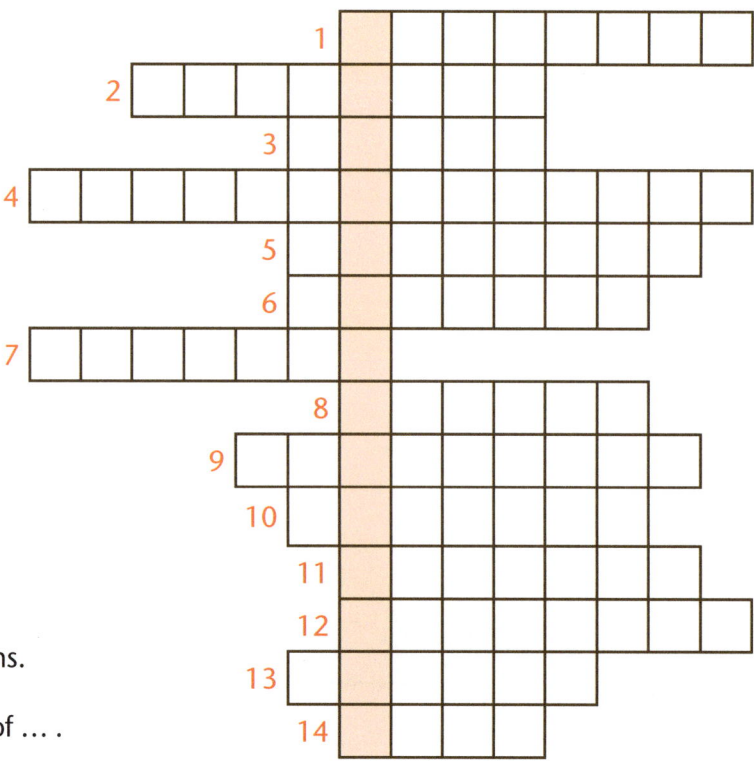

Raising animals and producing meat with mechanized methods: _____.

B6 ● A different way of farming

a) Read about organic* farming and fill in the passive form of the verbs.

On organic farms animals _____ (treat) much better than animals on factory farms. Cows and pigs _____ (keep) in huge green fields. When it is very cold, they _____ (put) into large sheds where they are able to move. The calves _____ (leave) with their mothers so they can drink their milk. Chickens _____ (not raise) in cages and they can always go outdoors. Animals on organic farms _____ (feed) only biologically grown food and they _____ (not give) any drugs. The farms _____ (check) regularly by special inspectors. Reports suggest that organic meat that _____ (produce and pack) either by farmers themselves or by organic meat companies is much healthier than other meat. If the animals _____ (kill) on the farms where they have spent their lives you can usually be sure that they _____ (not make) to suffer. If they _____ (take) to slaughterhouses, however, it is possible that they die like all the other animals from factory farms. Animal rights organizations say this _____ (must improve).

*organic – organisch, hier: Bio

b) Listen to the CD and check your text.

c) Compare the information above with the facts from B5 in your textbook. How is meat produced in organic and in factory farming? Make a list of the differences and present it.

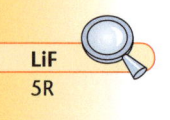

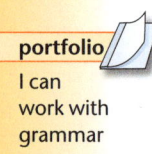

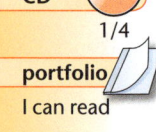

1 Meet the challenge

B7 ● The food they prefer

a) Fill in: either … or or neither … nor

1. Vegetarians eat _____ meat _____ fish.
2. A lot of them only put _____ cheese _____ jam[1] on their bread.
3. In our school cafeteria they _____ serve tofu hot dogs _____ vegetable burgers for vegetarians. Both dishes are good.
4. _____ Paula _____ Jill thinks it is OK to kill animals. So they have become vegetarians like Jamila.
5. One of the Marshalls is also a vegetarian, _____ Rick _____ Michelle, but I can't remember which of them.
6. _____ my parents _____ my brothers have ever tried tofu.
7. In your project on vegetarianism you can _____ do some research on people's reasons for not eating meat _____ on the food they prefer instead of meat and fish.
8. There are three vegetarian restaurants in town, *Veggie World, Greenfoods* and *Linda's Kitchen*. _____ *Veggie World* _____ *Greenfoods* is very good, but *Linda's Kitchen* is great.
9. If you go there, you should try _____ a vegetable pie _____ a Chinese soup.

b) Listen to the CD and check your sentences.

[1] jam – Marmelade

B8 ○ Meatless Monday

a) **Before reading:**
- Find Baltimore on a map of the USA.
- What kinds of food do *you* like? Could you do without any of them? Talk to a partner.

b) **Reading for gist:** Read the article. Then say in one or two sentences what it is about.

Just one day without

Around 30 million American students are served a hot lunch at school every day. Most of them eat chicken nuggets, hot dogs, hamburgers, French fries, pizza and other fast foods that may fill their stomachs, but are hardly healthy. Teachers and food experts have been worried about this for a long time because more and more kids have serious weight[1] problems.

In Baltimore a new school program was started in September 2009: Meatless Monday. On the first day of every week more than 80,000 schoolkids in the city have pasta, bean[2] dishes, fruit and vegetables, salads and cheese instead of meat for lunch. A lot of the meals are prepared from local produce.

Having a fresh and tasty lunch once a week has improved the diet of many schoolkids. It has also offered some students a chance to get to know foods they had never eaten before, especially vegetables. For others, sadly, it is the only healthy meal they receive all week.

The program has been a great success so far. Schools in other cities in the US have followed the example and have changed their Monday menus. Many universities, hospitals and restaurants start the week with a meat-free day, too.

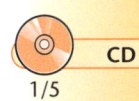

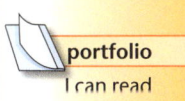

1 Meet the challenge

Improving health

Why Monday? Research shows that the beginning of the week is the best time for a fresh start. People are more willing[3] to start a diet, to begin exercising or to quit smoking on Monday than on any other day. And as most people have quite a few meat dishes on the weekend, they can more easily accept a vegetarian day after that. Why meatless? Eating a lot of meat can lead to different illnesses like heart disease and cancer, while eating a lot of vegetables can help to avoid health problems.

Can doing without meat just one day per week really make a big difference? Yes, it can – not only for your own health, but also for the health of the planet. If we all had meat-free Mondays, we would help to improve the environment in different ways:

- We would help to reduce greenhouse gases[4]. 13.5 to 18 per cent of these gases are produced by the animal industry.
- We would help to save water. Between 50,000 and 100,000 litres of water are needed to produce just one kilogram of beef.
- We would help to save trees, millions of which are cut each year. The land is made into fields where food for animals is grown – animals which are then eaten by us.
- We would help to improve the living conditions of animals because there would be fewer factory farms.

So what do you think, could you do without meat once a week?

[1] weight – *Gewicht;* [2] bean – *Bohne;* [3] willing – *bereit, gewillt;* [4] greenhouse gas – *Treibhausgas*

c) **Second reading:**
- First make a grid like this in your exercise book.

Type of question	Question	Answer	How I found the answer

- Read every question very carefully and think about how to find the answer:
    - Often you can find the information **in the text** – either in one word or in one sentence.
    - Sometimes there is no information in the text, so you need your **head**. This means that you have to use your background knowledge[1] and your experience[2] to find the answer.

- Work like this:
    1. Look at the keywords in the questions and try to find these words in the text. If you can't find them in the text, use your head.
    2. Underline the words or text passages[3] in which you find the information for the answer.
    3. Write the questions and answers into your grid. When you have answered a question, note down how you found the answer. Then write into the left column[4] which type of QAR question it is. Use your QAR cards for help.

Tip
You can fill in the right column in German.

- Now answer these questions.
    1. Why was Monday chosen for a meat-free day?
    2. What do American schoolkids usually have for lunch, and what kind of food is served on Meatless Monday?
    3. Why do you think the Meatless Monday program has been a success in Baltimore schools?
    4. Where else in the US has the campaign been started?
    5. Eating too much meat can be bad for your health. What three health problems are mentioned in the text?
    6. Eating meat every day is bad for our planet. Explain why.
    7. How could animals be raised if we all ate less meat?
    8. Answer the question at the end of the article. Give reasons.

- First compare your notes with a partner's, then compare them in class.

d) **After reading:** Write a Meatless Monday menu with a partner. Choose dishes that you would personally like to eat. Hang up your menus in class and talk about them.

[1] background knowledge – *Hintergrundwissen;* [2] experience – *Erfahrung;* [3] text passage – *Textabschnitt;* [4] column – *Spalte*

B9 ● Buying at farm shops: a good idea?

A British friend who is visiting you sees you reading this online article.

Ein Idyll?
Der Ausflug auf den Hofladen

Der Bio-Hof von Agnes und Wilhelm Timmermann ist eine Freude. Er liegt am Rande der Sülldorfer Feldmark im Westen Hamburgs, einem Naturschutzgebiet mit Pferdehöfen, Kühen und satten grünen Wiesen. Seit 20 Jahren wird hier nach den Vorgaben des Anbauverbandes Bioland Landwirtschaft betrieben.

Es gibt einen wunderbaren Hofladen unter Reetdach, in dem man Gemüse, Obst, Eier und Fleisch aus eigener Erzeugung einkaufen kann. Darüber hinaus findet man fast alle Lebensmittel für den täglichen Bedarf: Brot und Käse, Nudeln, Reis und Kartoffelpüree, Milchprodukte, Fertigprodukte, Wein, Säfte und sogar Eis.

Ein Besuch hier ist ein kleiner Ferientag für die ganze Familie. Die Kinder können im Heu toben, Kaninchen streicheln, zugucken, wenn die Hofschweine gefüttert werden, und die Hühner besuchen – während die Eltern in Ruhe einkaufen.

Manche Leute aus dem nahe gelegenen Sülldorf kommen per Rad oder zu Fuß mit Kinderwagen, um einzukaufen. Gerade am Wochenende aber ist der Hof manchmal voll mit Autos. Die kommen von überall her, aus Hamburg, aber auch aus Schleswig-Holstein, wie die Nummernschilder verraten.

In den zahlreichen Hofläden Deutschlands werden Gemüse, Obst, Eier oder Fleisch aus eigener Erzeugung verkauft. Ökologisch ist der Erlebniseinkauf meist aber nicht.

Doch ist es wirklich ökologisch sinnvoll, auf einen Bauernhof am Stadtrand oder gar auf die grüne Wiese zu fahren, um dort Lebensmittel einzukaufen?

Am günstigsten aus ökologischer Sicht ist es, in der eigenen Umgebung einzukaufen – auf dem Wochenmarkt und in nahe gelegenen Geschäften. Man sollte darauf achten, dass die Waren aus der Region stammen, also nicht von weither antransportiert wurden. Auch Supermärkte bieten inzwischen viele regionale Produkte an.

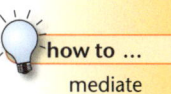

Answer your friend's questions.

- Nice photo! Where can you find that kind of shop?
- What can you buy there?
- Why are those shops so popular?
- So it's really good for everyone to buy their food there, isn't it?
- Where should people who live in the city buy their food instead?

☼ Explain to your friend why people should buy products from their area.

B10 ○ Choose

1. Work with a partner and make up a dialogue. You are both very hungry. Partner 1 wants to go to a vegetarian snack bar. Partner 2 would prefer a burger bar.
2. Work in a group. Write a short rap about vegetarian food and present it.
3. Draw a cartoon in which two animals talk about their life on a factory farm.
4. Write a diary entry for Lisa Simpson at the end of the day of her father's barbecue.

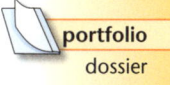

1 Detective page

D1 a) Match the verbs with these sports words.

> abseiling • extreme sports • bungee jumping • chess • parkour • karate • volleyball

do: _____

go: _____

play: _____

b) Find at least three more sports words that you can use with each verb.

D2 Fill in the lists.

adjective	noun
distant	
	environment
vegetarian	
	popularity
dangerous	
	nature

adjective	noun
healthy	
	adventure
safe	
	challenge
free	
	season

D3 a) Match the verbs with the prepositions. Draw lines.

stay   warm   keep   turn   stand   try   do   lie

around   for   without   out   away from   down   with   up

portfolio
I can work
with words

b) Now match the phrasal verbs from a) with the German translations. Write them down.

bedeuten –	ausprobieren –
sich hinlegen –	ohne etwas auskommen –
fernhalten von –	wohnen bei –
sich warm laufen –	sich umdrehen –

D4 Good to know …

When you're invited to dinner, make sure to always be polite about the food. Never say that a dish is not nice, rather say it is interesting. It is absolutely OK to say so if you don't like something – as long as you're polite.

16

A1 • A job crossword

a) Fill in the English words.

Down:
1. Unterkunft
3. Erfahrung
4. Lohn
5. freiwillig
9. Büro

Across:
2. Bewerbung
6. Vorstellungsgespräch
7. Teilzeit
8. zuverlässig
10. ehrlich
11. Geschäft
12. Stelle
13. Gelegenheit

b) Now use the words from the crossword to complete the sentences.

1. Before you are given a job, you must write an _____.
2. If they think you are a good candidate, you are invited to come for an _____ in which you talk about the _____ you have had so far.
3. Someone who wants to work in a hotel, a B&B or a holiday home must be _____ and never take any of the guests' things.
4. You must also be very _____ and always do what you are told.
5. When doing such a job, you usually get free _____ and food.
6. Don't expect much money. People doing work experience only receive a small _____.
7. In some jobs you might only have to work _____, perhaps four or five hours a day.
8. An _____ is a room where people work sitting at desks, using computers and telephones.
9. It can be quite good to work in a small _____ because the boss will often give you a variety of tasks and you will learn a lot.
10. A _____ job is a _____ for which you don't get any money.
11. Any student who wants to work with people from other countries should try to find a summer job in Britain because it is a great _____ to improve your English.

A2 ● Job offers on the Internet

a) Read the job adverts in A2 in your textbook again. Tick right, wrong or not in the text.

	right	wrong	not in the text
1. Most guests at the B&B in Brighton are from abroad.	☐	☐	☐
2. You have one free afternoon if you have a summer job at the B&B.	☐	☐	☐
3. Several candidates can do the work experience at the Olympic Committee Press Office as volunteers for three months.	☐	☐	☐
4. For two of them there will be a paid position after the work experience.	☐	☐	☐
5. They will work in a big office building.	☐	☐	☐
6. The job at the breeding kennels is a live-in position for three months and you get full board and lodging.	☐	☐	☐
7. If you work at the breeding kennels, you often have to take the dogs for a walk.	☐	☐	☐
8. If you are interested in working at the vineyard, you have to stay at least four weeks.	☐	☐	☐
9. You have to be 18 years old to do the job at the vineyard.	☐	☐	☐

b) Correct the sentences that are wrong. Write them into your exercise book.

A3 ● Working in Britain

You want to go to Britain to do a work placement for a few weeks and have found this website, which organizes such placements. You call your dad, who is at work at the moment, and tell him in German what you have found out.

- Explain to him where you could work and what kind of work you could do.
- Give examples of how the organization Twin would help you.

Then explain what qualifications you must have.

---

http://www.workuk.co.uk/Programme/?pgid=26

The organization Twin offers you the opportunity to try out a career and improve your English at the same time. We will find you a work placement and an English language course in either London or Eastbourne. We offer placements in many different areas of work.

To apply you must be at least 16 and have an intermediate level of English. When you apply, you should say which area of work interests you the most and how long you would like to work and study for. You can start on any Monday throughout the year.

What we offer you in England:
- From 1 week to 4 weeks English language course
- From 2 weeks to 24 weeks work placement
- Personalised programme based on your career plans and language ability
- Accommodation in families
- Pick up from the airport
- Introduction to fellow travellers of all nationalities through our social programme
- Sightseeing trips and activities
- Travel cards
- 24 hour emergency support
- Certificate and final report from place of work

A4 ● How to make a CV shine

a) The "key skills" section is a very important part in a CV because it shows whether someone is the right person for a job.

Look at these words and phrases. Which key skills are needed in different jobs? Match them with the jobs in the list. Many of them are needed in more than one job.

> good manual skills • good team working skills • excellent communication skills • good command of foreign languages • good at using standard office software • able to work with a variety of people • able to work without help or supervision • able to write information down accurately • able to check and correct mistakes • able to analyse and solve problems • good knowledge of biology

Job	Key skills needed for the job
office worker	
doctor's assistant	
salesperson	
car technician	
police officer	
your future work experience: _____	

b) Compare your findings with a partner's.

- A salesperson needs … because they …
- That's right. And they must also …
- Car technicians often … That's why they have to be able to …

c) Add key skills that you need for your future work experience. Use them when writing your CV in A3c) in your textbook.

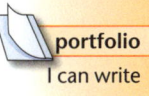

2 Off to work

A5 • Two letters

a) Look at Nadira's letter from A3d) in your textbook again. Find the English translations for these German phrases.

1. Sehr geehrte Damen und Herren,
   _____

2. Ich möchte mich um eine Stelle im Mai bewerben.
   _____

3. Ich füge meinen Lebenslauf bei.
   _____

4. Das Praktikum würde mir die Gelegenheit bieten, wichtige Arbeitserfahrungen in einem beruflichen Umfeld machen zu können.
   _____

5. Für ein Vorstellungsgespräch stehe ich jederzeit zur Verfügung.
   _____

6. Für die Berücksichtigung meiner Bewerbung bedanke ich mich.
   _____

7. Ich freue mich darauf, bald von Ihnen zu hören.
   _____

8. Mit freundlichen Grüßen
   _____

b) Jason, Nadira's neighbour, wants to apply for a work experience placement in a computer shop. He wrote a letter but it isn't very good. Which parts shouldn't be in it? Cross them out in red.

Jason Burroughs
Hendon

Hendon Computers
7–9 High Street
London

Hello,
I want to do my work experience in your shop because it is a really cool place. ☺
I will finish school this year. Then I want to go on holiday. I don't have much experience selling things but I like learning new things. I am very interested in computers and spend a lot of time on mine after school. I am a friendly and enthusiastic person and I also enjoy working in a team. I've always wanted to work with people.
As you will see from my CV, I have been volunteering in an animal shelter since last year.
I hope I don't have to work after 6 pm because I am always very tired in the evening. But perhaps if the pay is good, then it will be OK on a few evenings per month.
I am available for an interview at any time. Write back soon!
Bye,

Jason Burroughs

---

how to…
write a letter of application

c) Now check the language. Which parts do you have to change? Mark them in green.

d) Mark in blue where you have to add further information.

portfolio
I can write

e) Write a new letter for Jason in your exercise book or type it on the computer. Use phrases from a) and make up further information that is needed to make a good impression.

Off to work **2**

A6 ○ Choose

1. Interview an older student, someone in your family or another person who has already done work experience. Take notes and report to the class. Say

    – where and when the person did work experience.
    – what he or she had to do in the job.
    – whether he or she liked the job.
    – whether you can imagine doing work experience at the same place.

2. Make a poster or presentation about a job you would like to do.

    – Show pictures or photos.
    – Explain what you have to do in the job.
    – Then say why you think it would be a good job for you.

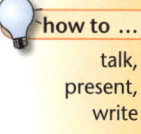

3. Choose one of the jobs from A2 in your textbook and write a letter of application. Then swap it with a partner's. Edit each other's letters.

4. Write **your** letter of application for the work experience you have chosen. Then swap it with a partner's letter. Edit each other's letters.

how to …
talk, present, write

wordbank
jobs

portfolio
I can combine skills, learn English

portfolio
dossier

A7 ● Jeff's talk

a) Jeff, one of Nadira's classmates, did his work experience in a coffee shop. Back at school he gives a short talk to his class. What does he say? Listen and take notes.

- reason for application: _____
- working hours: _____
- manager & other people working at the place: _____
  _____
- jobs: _____
  _____
- what he enjoyed: _____

CD 1/8

how to …
listen

b) Report what Jeff says in his talk.

Jeff says he applied _____
He says work started _____
He says _____
_____
_____
_____
_____
_____

portfolio
I can listen, work with grammar

LiF
7R

21

2 Off to work

A8 ● Her biggest dream

a) What happened before Nadira did her work experience? Why has she always wanted to be a hairdresser? Use your imagination and add at least three ideas to this timeline.

went to the hairdresser's with her mother for the first time as a little girl → decided it was the perfect job for her →

→ did work experience at Director's Cut Hairdressing Salon

b) Write about your timeline, using "after" or "before".

After Nadira had gone

A9 ● Other work experience

a) Write down what other people said about their work experience.

1. Tricia: "I did my work experience in the local library."

Tricia said she had done

2. Joshua: "I got a placement in a small sports shop."

Joshua said he

3. Grace: "Working in a kindergarten was good fun because the kids were lovely."

4. Dylan: "I spent the two weeks in a bakery and got up early every morning."

5. Sumati: "I didn't like my boss because he shouted at me all the time."

6. Mia: "I worked in a supermarket, but I wasn't allowed to help customers."

7. Owen: "I was very tired when I finished my job in a hospital."

8. Halim: "I did my work experience at the local police station and I really enjoyed the work I was doing there."

b) Listen to the CD and check your sentences.

Off to work **2**

A10 ● When?

a) **Tick the right time expressions.**

1. When we met Jasmine in town last week she said that she had finished her work experience
   ☐ yesterday.   ☐ the day before.
2. She explained that she had started the job   ☐ two weeks earlier.   ☐ two weeks ago.
3. She told us that she had taken a car apart for the first time   ☐ a week ago.
   ☐ the week before.
4. She said that she had to give a talk about her job at school   ☐ the next day.   ☐ tomorrow.
5. She was in a hurry and said that she still had so much to do   ☐ today.   ☐ that day.

b) **Listen to the CD and check your sentences.**
c) **Write down what Jasmine said.**

1. <u>Jasmine: "I finished my work experience</u> _____
2. _____
3. _____
4. _____
5. _____

☼ Look at the time expressions in a) and c). What do you notice?
_____

A11 ○ Jasmine's plans

a) Before Jasmine does her work experience, she talks to two friends about her plan to apply for a job in a local garage. What does she say? How do her friends react? Work in groups of three. Continue the dialogue together.

Jasmine: Listen, I'm going to do my work experience in a garage. Isn't that great?

Friend 1: Ugh, in a garage? How awful! You will get dirty hands.

Jasmine: What's wrong with getting dirty hands? _____

Friend 2: _____
Jasmine: _____
Friend 1: _____
Jasmine: _____
Friend 2: _____
Jasmine: _____
Friend 1: _____
Friend 2: _____
Jasmine: _____

b) ⭐ Practise reading your dialogue and then act it out.

☼ Learn the dialogue by heart and act it out in class.

2 Off to work

B1 ⭘ Your soft skills

a) What are your soft skills? What are your partner's soft skills? Write down three for each of you. Note down examples, too.

My soft skills	Examples

My partner's soft skills	Examples

portfolio
I can work with words

b) Tell your partner what you think his / her soft skills are. Say why.

c) Do you agree with your partner's opinion of you? How do you see yourself? Compare his / her ideas with your own.

> I think you are very … because you always / often …

> You are … because you can … For example, you …

B2 ● Good advice

What information or advice would you give these young people? Write down tips for them. Use the ideas from the box or your own ideas.

> talk to teacher about talents • be very reliable • consider becoming a coach • check message boards in local supermarkets • have better chances of finding a job • improve Spanish • be interested in Biology, Chemistry and Physics

1. Amy isn't sure how many applications for work experience placements she should write.
   If you write four or five applications, you will _____

2. Dean would like a weekend job, but he doesn't know how to find one.
   If you want a weekend job, you should _____

3. Sarah doesn't know if babysitting is the right thing for her.
   If you are a babysitter, you have to _____

4. Rick has no idea what kind of job would be good for him.
   _____

5. James isn't sure what qualifications he needs to work in a laboratory.
   _____

6. Evie would like to work abroad in the summer, but she can't decide where to apply.
   _____

7. Robert needs a part-time job. He enjoys working with children and doing sports.
   _____

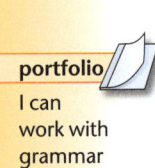

LiF 10R

portfolio
I can work with grammar

Off to work

B3 ● Phoning for a job

a) Three people are phoning to find out more about a job. Listen to their phone calls and take notes in this grid. Write an ✗ if there is no information.

	Emily	Mary	Eric
job			
job advert: where?			
working hours			
weekend work?			
team: how big?			
soft skills			
money / salary			
work experience			
job interview: when?			
start of work: when?			

how to …
listen, talk

portfolio
I can listen

b) Choose one person. Use your notes to give a talk about the job he or she wants to have.

c) Look at the different soft skills that the people need. Explain why these soft skills are important for the jobs.

B4 ● How to say it

Listen to the phone calls in B3 above and answer these questions.

1. Wie fragt Debbie von *Debbie's Hairdreams*, ob Emily schon Erfahrung hat?
   _____

2. Wie sagt sie, dass momentan fünf Leute in ihrem Friseursalon arbeiten?
   _____

3. Wie sagt Peggy von *Peggy's Boutique*, dass die Arbeitszeit von 15 bis 20 Uhr ist?
   _____

4. Wie fragt Mary, wann sie zum Vorstellungsgespräch in *Peggy's Boutique* kommen soll?
   _____

5. Wie sagt der Leiter des Fitness-Studios, dass es gut klingt, was Eric über sich berichtet?
   _____

portfolio
I can learn English

Use some of the phrases above in your phone call from B3 c) in your textbook.

25

2 Off to work

B5 ⭕ Choose

1. Cut out a job advert from your local newspaper and tell your partner about it in English. He / she takes notes and then tells the class in German what the advert is about.

wordbank — jobs

2. Write an advert for a job in your neighbourhood, at your sports club, at your youth club, … It can be a funny advert, too.

3. Work with a partner. Choose one soft skill, for example "being flexible". Act out a sketch in which a person shows that he or she has that soft skill.

B6 ⬤ Who is the right candidate?

a) Here are two letters written by young people who would like to do an apprenticeship at Daly's Garage. Mark each person's qualifications for the job.

Dear Mr Daly,

I read your advert at apprenticeships.co.uk and would like to apply for the job of apprentice car technician at your garage. I have enclosed my CV and the addresses of two people who can send you references.

I finished school two months ago after I had passed nine GCSEs. I got top marks in both Design Technology and Computer Science. I would be able to start work next month.

Cars and engines are my hobby. I always help my brother to repair his old car. I love repairing things and seeing them work again. I also love solving problems. I did my work experience in a car factory. I learned a lot during that time and enjoyed working in a team. The team leader was pleased with my work. At the moment I am learning to drive a car and ride a motorbike.

I can come for an interview at any time. Thank you for considering my application. I look forward to hearing from you soon.
Yours sincerely,

Daniel Jackson
Daniel Jackson

---

how to … — read

portfolio — I can read, learn English

Dear Sir,

I saw your advert for an apprenticeship as a car technician on the Internet. If you are still looking for a candidate, I hope you will consider my application.

I have just finished school and have got eight GCSEs with good results in English, Maths, Geography, and Computer Science. My hobbies are playing chess and repairing things such as old computers, old telephones, broken bicycles and broken furniture.

I did my work experience in a small computer repair shop where I learned about fixing PCs and laptops. At the end of the work experience I was also allowed to help customers. My boss said I was flexible and able to solve technical problems. She is prepared to act as a referee.

I am available for an interview at any time and look forward to hearing from you soon.
Yours sincerely,

C. Green
Colin Green

---

b) Now use a different colour to mark each person's soft skills.

portfolio — I can read

c) Look at Sarosh's CV in B4 in your textbook again and compare it with the two letters above. Who is the right candidate for the job? Discuss in class. Then take a vote.

Off to work **2**

B7 ○ FAQs about job interviews

a) A lot of teenagers are very nervous before their first job interview. Here are some frequently asked questions:

- How can I keep cool?
- What should I do if I can't answer a question?
- What kind of clothes should I wear?
- How can I prepare for the interview?

Now report what young candidates are often worried about.

A lot of young candidates want to know how they _____
They wonder what they _____
They ask themselves _____
_____

LiF 7R

b) Write down three questions **you** have about job interviews.

c) Tell the class what you would like to know about job interviews. Can the others give you tips or advice?

I'd like to know / I wonder …

B8 ○ How to make a good impression

a) What should you do to make a good impression in a job interview? And what shouldn't you do?

★ Look at the picture and write down at least eight tips for candidates.

☼ Look at the picture. Write down at least eight tips for candidates and give reasons.

You should / shouldn't … because …

You can use these ideas:

> clothes • be prepared • mobile phone • be on time • look at interviewer • sit straight • …

You should _____
You shouldn't _____
_____
_____
_____
_____
_____

LiF 4R

portfolio
I can work with grammar

b) Look at the picture again. What do you think the interviewer says about the candidate after the interview?

B9 • Interviews

a) Work with a partner and act out the scene. Partner A is the owner of a computer shop and partner B wants to get a Saturday job in the shop.

A: Inhaber des Computergeschäfts	B: Bewerber/in
Frage B,	Antworte A,
– ob er/sie schon einmal in einem Geschäft gearbeitet hat.	– dass du schon einmal ein Praktikum in einem Sportgeschäft gemacht hast.
– wie lange sein/ihr Praktikum dauerte.	– dass es zwei Wochen dauerte.
– wie viele Stunden er/sie täglich gearbeitet hat.	– dass du sechs Stunden am Tag gearbeitet hast.
– was er/sie gemacht hat.	– dass du Produkte sortiert und mit Kunden gesprochen hast.
– ob er/sie einen Computer benutzt hat.	– dass du einen Computer benutzt hast, um die Produkte zu zählen.
– ob ihm/ihr die Arbeit gefallen hat.	– dass dir die Arbeit sehr gefallen hat.
– was ihm/ihr am meisten Spaß gemacht hat.	– dass du am liebsten Kunden beraten hast.

portfolio — I can talk

b) After the interview the candidate's friend wants to know what questions the owner of the computer shop asked. Write down what the candidate reports.

Well, first the boss asked me if I had ever worked in a shop before.
Then he wanted to know _____
He also asked me _____
_____
_____
_____
_____

LiF 8R, 11

portfolio — I can work with grammar

B10 ○ Better luck next time!

Sarosh was really disappointed when he found out that he didn't get the job at Daly's Garage. His mum felt sorry for him. Write down what she said after Mr Daly had called.

Sarosh's mum asked why Mr Daly hadn't wanted to give Sarosh the job.
"Why didn't Mr Daly want _____

She asked Sarosh if he thought that Mr Daly hadn't liked him.
"Do you think _____

She said it was hard to find a job at a garage where you didn't have to work on Saturdays.
_____

She wanted to know whether Sarosh had seen any other adverts for interesting jobs.
_____

She told him his CV had been very good so he could use it again.
_____

LiF 9R, 11

Tip
If you like, you can change the order of the sentences from a) in your dialogue.

💡 What do you think Sarosh answered? Write the whole dialogue into your exercise book. Add further ideas to make the dialogue sound natural.

B11 ● Sound check

a) Say these words.

application	stamina	available	education	variety
surname	volunteer	regular	apprenticeship	layout
engineer	reliable	independent	necessary	address

b) Is the stress on the first, on the second or on the third syllable? Write the words into the right list.

stress on the first syllable	stress on the second syllable	stress on the third syllable

c) Listen to the CD and check your lists.

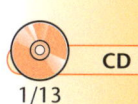

B12 ○ The call centre business

a) **Before reading:** What do you know about the work at call centres? Collect ideas in class.

b) **Reading for gist:** Read the text. Say in one or two sentences why so many people work in call centres.

The first call centres were opened in the USA, but it was in Britain in the 1970s that they really became successful. Companies decided that it was better if most telephone calls were made in one single office. Nowadays over 950,000 people are employed by call centres in the UK, and many more offices are being opened all over the world.

The first call centres were set up[1] in the financial sector[2], but others quickly followed. Nowadays a huge range of business sectors, such as travel and computer support, offer this kind of telephone service. One group of agents answers calls from customers. They take orders, answer questions, solve problems and provide information. Other agents call customers in order to sell products, make appointments or collect information about consumer habits. Call centres are often available for free – 24 hours a day, seven days a week. About 70% of the agents are female.

In regions with high unemployment[3], call centres are a chance for thousands of workers to get back on the job market. However, these jobs are more and more seen as stopgaps[4] rather than as careers.

You will often find call centres far away from the expensive industrial regions because employers have lower costs when setting them up and can pay lower wages.

(article continues on next page)

2 Off to work

This also explains the growing number of call centres in poor areas of India and Eastern Europe where both land and skilled labour[5] are cheap. In these countries even many qualified people don't have any alternatives to working in a call centre and are happy to receive a regular salary.

In some industries, however, call centres take away jobs. In banking, for example, customers are encouraged to use the telephone rather than actually go to their bank. Many banks have had to cut jobs and close branches[6].

Although call centre agents seem to be white-collar workers[7], their working conditions are much more like those of blue-collar workers[8]: productivity bonuses[9], round-the-clock shift work and overtime are normal. Their job is extremely stressful[10]: calls must be answered within a certain number of seconds, the conversation must be kept as short as possible, and all the agents have flashing[11] lights in front of them which tell them that more calls are waiting. A lot of customers call to complain about products or services. It often happens that they are extremely impolite to the agents, shout at them or even call them names. The conditions for part-time agents are the worst. Sometimes they work up to five hours without a break.

People in this business often have health problems. A lot of agents suffer from backache, coughs, sore throat[12] and breathing problems. Some even lose their voices. So it is no surprise that employees usually only stay in the industry for two years.

"Call centres are very important for customers' opinions of a company", says a former agent. "So why don't they do more to help their staff to feel comfortable in their job?

[1] set up – *aufbauen;* [2] sector – *Sektor, Bereich, Branche;* [3] unemployment – *Arbeitslosigkeit;* [4] stopgap – *Notlösung;* [5] labour – *ausgebildete Arbeitskräfte;* [6] branch – *Zweigstelle;* [7] white-collar worker – *(Büro)Angestellte/r;* [8] blue-collar worker – *Fabrikarbeiter/in;* [9] productivity bonus – *Leistungszulage;* [10] stressful – *stressig, anstrengend;* [11] flashing – *aufleuchtend, zuckend;* [12] sore throat – *Halsschmerzen*

---

c) Second reading:
- First make a grid like this in your exercise book.

Type of question	Question	Answer	How I found the answer

Tip
Look at pages 13 and 14 in this workbook for help with QAR again.

- Answer these questions, using the QAR strategy. Your QAR cards will be helpful.

1. What are the tasks of call centre agents?
2. How long do most of them stay in the job?
3. What is the special service of call centres?
4. Why is the job of a call centre agent stressful?
5. Where did the call centre industry start, and how has it developed since then?
6. What advantages do companies have when they set up call centres in poor regions or countries?
7. You will find a lot of people with high qualifications working in Indian call centres. Why don't they take other jobs?
8. Why do you think most call centre agents are female?
9. In what ways has the banking sector suffered from the call centre industry?
10. What are the working conditions of white-collar workers like?
11. Why are call centre agents more like blue-collar workers?
12. If you really needed a job, would you work in a call centre? Say why or why not.

- First compare your notes with a partner's, then compare them in class.

d) Find a good title and write it above the text.

e) After reading: Work with a partner. How could call centres improve their agents' working conditions? Collect ideas and compare them in class.

Off to work **2**

B13 ● A virtual job fair

a) Listen to the CD and number the pictures in the right order.

CD
1/12

portfolio
I can listen

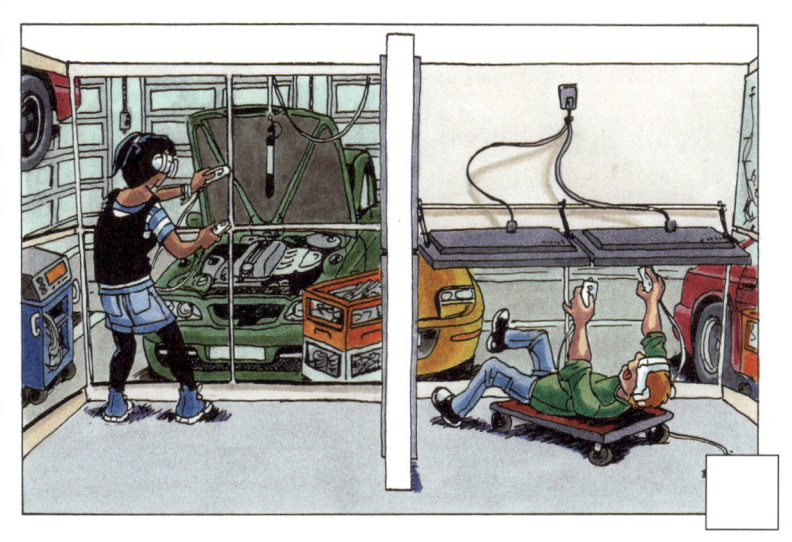

b) Listen again. What is special about the different job tests? Take notes.

c) ★ Which job or jobs would **you** like to try out? Say why.

☀ Describe each job test in a few sentences. Say which job **you** would like to try out and why.

31

Detective page

D1 Fill in the lists.

verb	noun
apply	
	advice
know	
	start

verb	noun
solve	
	interview
repair	
	change

D2 Write down words that mean the same.

position	
salary	
opportunity	
ring up	
search for	

location	
renowned	
last name	
on time	
bit	

D3 Complete the definitions with new words from the theme.

1. If you _____ with people, you express thoughts, feelings or information.
2. People who are _____ can do things on their own without any help.
3. An _____ is a meeting or a visit at a particular time.
4. People who have _____ don't give up easily.
5. Correct _____ is the correct way of writing words.

D4 Match the verbs with the nouns.

do • enclose • apply for • book • make • solve • get • be used to • change • give • arrange • join

a CV • a hotel • wheels • problems • a career • a team • appointments • hard work • experience • work experience • feedback • a position

D5 Good to know …

Applying for a job works differently in different countries. In America, Australia and the UK people do not put a photo on their CV. It is also unusual to include reports from school or university. References from former employers or teachers are much more important.

Express yourself **3**

Projects 1–4 ● Before you start

a) Think about your experiences with projects you have done in the last few years. Make notes.

_____
_____
_____

What do you like about projects?

_____
_____

What don't you like about projects?

_____
_____

b) **Talk about your answers in your project group.**

portfolio
I can talk

c) What do you expect from the project you will be doing in this Theme? Think of team work, results, fun, difficulties, … Collect ideas in your group and make notes.

_____
_____
_____
_____

Project 1 ● Music and attitudes

a) Look up in a dictionary what the phrase "white lie" means in German.

white lie – _____

b) Read the portrait of White Lies and listen to a student presenting it. Then look up new words in a dictionary and read the portrait a second time.

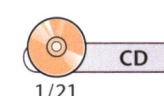

CD 1/21

portfolio
I can read, listen

Today I'm going to talk about the *White Lies*, who are one of my favourite bands at the moment.
They are an alternative rock band from London. I really like their dark sound and their poetic lyrics.
The band members are Harry McVeigh, Charles Cave and Jack Lawrence-Brown. McVeigh is the lead singer and plays the guitar, Cave plays the bass guitar and sings backing vocals and Lawrence-Brown plays the drums.
The three musicians started playing music together under the name *Fear of Flying* when they were 15 and still going to school. They completed one UK tour as a support act and produced two singles.

(article continues on next page)

3
Express yourself

> In 2007 they formed the *White Lies*, introducing a new, much darker sound. Why did they choose this name? "Because white lies are common but quite dark, and that's how we see ourselves," they once explained. Some of their songs are about death, others are about feelings that most people experience at some point in their life, like feelings about losing a person you love. But even though the subjects of the songs are often serious or sad, the music itself is mostly pretty upbeat.
>
> A lot of young people identify with *White Lies*' songs, which is why the band has become really popular. After they had released their first two singles, "Unfinished Business" and "Death", they went on tours in the UK and North America. In January 2009 they released their first album, *To Lose My Life,* which was number one in the UK Albums Chart. They also won three awards in 2009 and 2010. Their second album *Ritual* was released in January 2011.
>
> I often watch *White Lies*' videos on the Internet and I think Harry McVeigh's voice is just amazing. I hope I'll be able to go to one of their concerts some time.
>
> If you are interested in their music, you should have a look at their website www.whitelies.com. You will find great videos and a lot of information about the band on it.
>
> Well, that was my presentation on the band *White Lies*. I hope you liked it. If you have any questions, please feel free to ask me. Thank you very much for your attention.

portfolio
I can work with words

c) Do you think the band is presented in an interesting way? Say why or why not.

d) Look at the text again and find phrases to describe bands. Sort the phrases into this grid.

roles of band members	lead singer,
music style	
lyrics	
attitude and image	
career	

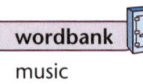

wordbank
music

e) Work with a partner. Find more phrases you can use to present bands or singers. Add them to the grid above.

f) With your project group, collect all the phrases you find useful on a poster. They are your project words.

Express yourself **3**

Projects 1 and 3 ○ Being different

a) Choose one of the people shown in the photos and make notes.

A B C

Give the person a name. _____

What do you think is his/her family background? _____

_____

Who are his/her friends? _____

_____

What are his/her hobbies and free time activities? _____

_____

Why did he/she choose this kind of appearance? _____

_____

portfolio
I can write

b) How do you think different people react to the way the person looks?

Family: _____

_____

Friends: _____

_____

Teachers: _____

_____

People in the street: _____

_____

c) How do the different reactions make the person feel? Collect phrases.

_____

_____

d) What do you think of the person?

_____

_____

e) Talk to a classmate who chose the same person. Compare your ideas.

35

Project 2 ○ A profile

a) Read the portrait of hip hop singer Dessa. Look up new words in a dictionary.

There aren't many successful female rappers in the music industry, so hip hop singer Dessa stands out. She started writing poetry after finishing university. Her poetry caught the attention of rapper MC Yoni, and together with two other musicians they formed the group Medida. Dessa learned a lot from MC Yoni, and he also introduced her to the Doomtree collective, a group of rappers and hip hop musicians. Between 2005 and 2008 she appeared on many Doomtree albums.

In 2005 she released the EP *False Hopes*. In early 2010 she released her first solo album, *A Badly Broken Code*. Dessa has many talents: she is a great poet, thoughtful songwriter, great singer and clever MC. She also sings with *The Boy Sopranos*, an a capella group, and she has two teaching jobs, one of them at a music college. In the last few years her fame has grown, and she is now very popular not just in her home town of Chicago, but right across the USA.

b) Use information from the portrait to fill in the fact file.

Name: **Dessa** _____

Lives in: _____

Music styles: _____

Jobs: _____

Career: _____

Other information: _____

c) Use your fact file to talk about Dessa. Practise this silently.

d) Now tell a partner about Dessa.

Project 2 ○ Hip hop language

a) There are lots of special words in hip hop lyrics. Here are some of them. Do you know what they mean? Talk to a partner. Try to guess if you aren't sure.

mo'   payce   dat   flow
'sup   sitch   phat   hella
aight   roll out   po'   dis   cuz   boyz

b) Match the words in these lists with the hip hop expressions from a).

hip hop slang	
this	
that	
more	
because	
all right	
rap	
situation	

hip hop slang	
gang friends	
What's up?	
very cool	
peace	
hell of	
poor	
leave	

c) Listen to the CD and check your lists.

d) Read about the four important elements of hip hop. Look up new words in a dictionary.

_____ is a special technique used by DJs. They produce sounds by moving a record back and forth on a record player.

_____ means speaking or chanting lyrics that rhyme.

Producing drum beats, rhythms, and musical sounds using the mouth, lips, tongue and voice is called _____.

_____ means taking one part of a recording and then using it in another song. This is usually done with a sampler, which can be hardware or a computer programme.

e) Add the names of the four important elements of hip hop to the explanations from d).

beatboxing   DJing (Scratching)   sampling   rapping (emceeing)

f) Make a poster about hip hop language. Use the expressions and explanations on this page and find more phrases.

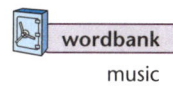

wordbank: music

3

Express yourself

Project 3 ○ Describing comics

a) Work in a group and talk about these comic covers. Which of the comics would you like to read? Give reasons.

… looks really interesting / exciting because …

… is the kind of story I like.

… is probably about …

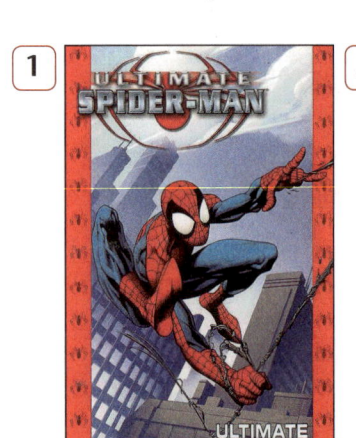

portfolio — I can talk

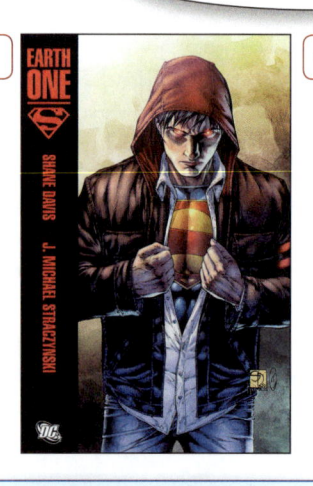

1. Ultimate Spider-Man
2. Alichino
3. Earth One (Superman)
4. Fruits Basket

wordbank — comic

b) Write down phrases to describe the cover that you like best. The words from the box might be helpful.

- drawing style: realistic / photo-like / original / …
- use of colour: bright / dark / … colours
- figure(s) shown: realistic / superhuman / fantasy / …
- face: scary / sad / … • interesting details: …

portfolio — I can work with words

_____
_____
_____
_____
_____
_____

portfolio — I can read

c) Read the extracts from summaries of the comics and match them with the covers from a).

A ☐ Kyo tells Tohru about his role in her mother's death, which is why he went away for a long time. Tohru tells him that she still loves him but he says the wrong thing. She runs off and something terrible happens.

B ☐ The comic presents the famous superhero in a way you've always known him – and yet completely differently. In this new version of the story the character who could formerly be easily identified by his blue, red and yellow costume is presented as a normal guy who "doesn't want to stand out."

C ☐ The story is about beautiful demons who have the power to grant wishes. Therefore humans are attracted to them. But for every wish the demons grant, they want a soul in return. The first volume focuses on the young boy Tsugiri, who knows their dark secret and who has to fight the demons in order to rescue a girl …

D ☐ In this collection you can read about the important year that changed the life of Peter Parker, the shy high-school student who turned into a superhero after he had been bitten by a radioactive spider.

portfolio — I can read, combine skills

d) Work with a partner and describe the comic you think is the most intereresting. Use your ideas from b) and some information from c).

38

Express yourself **3**

Project 4 ● Fashion and style

a) Talk to a partner. Which style or styles do you like best? Say why.

1   2   3   4
5   6   7   8

portfolio
I can talk

b) Make a list of the people's clothes and accessories. Use a dictionary.

_____
_____
_____
_____
_____

wordbank
fashion

portfolio
I can work with words

c) Choose two people, one male and one female, and answer the questions.

- What do the people look like (trendy, cool, stylish, conservative, …)?
- What do they want to express with the way they look?
- How do you think they feel about their style?

<u>The young man in photo number</u>   : _____
_____
_____

<u>The young woman in photo number</u>   : _____
_____
_____

d) Form a group with classmates who have described different people. Together make a word field like this about fashion. Use your ideas from b) and c).

portfolio
I can work with words

Fashion					
clothes	fashion accessories	hairstyles	what people look like	what people want to express through fashion	how people feel about their styles

39

3

Express yourself

Project 4 ○ A fashion show

a) Sara's class organized a fashion show at school. Read her report and look up new words.

A fashion show at our school

We're in year 9 and did a great project last week. On the last afternoon of our project week we presented a fashion show in English. It took place in the school hall in front of the whole school. Preparing the fashion show was hard work but also a lot of fun. We started with a planning session in which we collected ideas and distributed tasks. There were so many things to do and consider! This is what we had to do before we could present our designs on the catwalk:
first of all we looked at lots of fashion magazines and fashion brochures. Then we went through our parents' and even our grandparents' wardrobes. We asked our sisters, brothers, neighbours and teachers to lend us clothes. And we searched our homes for stuff that could be recycled and used in a creative way, like plastic bags in different colours and sizes, ribbons, feathers, and small coloured kitchen sponges.
We combined new and old clothes and came up with some really good ideas for accessories. Two people in our group know how to use a sewing machine and they changed the clothes for us so that they fitted really well.
Everyone had to write texts about the clothes they designed. The presenters used these texts for their announcements, which they had to learn by heart. The models practised walking down the catwalk. Only the girls in our group wanted to be models and even had to present men's fashion because the boys were too shy. They preferred to be the presenters.
Of course we also had to choose some cool music for our show. We had long discussions about this because our tastes in music are quite different, but we finally agreed on some pop songs you can easily move and dance to.
Although we rehearsed several times, checking each other's parts and giving each other tips, we were still very nervous before our show in the school hall. But it went extremely well. The audience clapped and cheered a lot. The highlight of the show was our presentation of our teachers' evening and wedding dresses. Pupils who guessed the owners won a prize. When the show was over we were really proud that it had been such a great success.

b) Underline words and phrases for the different jobs the project group had to do.

c) What did the group have to do in the different phases of the project? Make lists like these in your exercise book. Sort the words that you underlined into the lists.

Phase 1: Plan it	Phase 2: Do it	Phase 3: Check it	Phase 4: Present it

d) Listen to the recordings from the fashion show and tick the phrases you hear.

- ☐ Let's give a big hand to … !
- ☐ Welcome to our fashion show!
- ☐ … some of the hottest fashion trends from our summer collection.
- ☐ Coming down the catwalk now is …
- ☐ Doesn't she / he look …
- ☐ And look at how well the … goes with the …
- ☐ What an eyecatcher!
- ☐ This season's colour …
- ☐ Please welcome our first model …
- ☐ His / her shirt / trousers / skirt is / are made of …
- ☐ … is an absolute must this season!

Tip
You can listen again and note down more useful phrases for your own fashion show.

e) Do you like the way Sara's class presented their fashion show? Say why or why not. What would *you* do in the same way? What would *you* do differently?

Express yourself **3**

Projects 1–4 ○ Collecting ideas

a) Collect ideas for your project. What do you want to do? Make notes.

_____

_____

_____

_____

_____

b) Compare your ideas in your project group. Agree on the ideas you like best and make a new list.

portfolio
I can talk

Ideas for our project:

- _____
- _____
- _____
- _____
- _____
- _____

Projects 1–4 ○ Distributing tasks

a) Who wants to do what for your project? Fill in the list.

portfolio
I can talk

name	task	done?

b) During your project, tick each task that has been done.

3 Express yourself

how to …
present

Projects 1–4 ○ Phrases for presentations

a) Here are some useful phrases for presentations. Write them into the right list.

> So, to summarise … • Today I'm going to talk about … • Do you see what I mean? • First of all, I'm going to … • So let's start with … • Thank you for listening. • Then I'll talk about … • Finally I'll … • That's why … • Don't you agree? • Let's look at … • Please feel free to interrupt me. • So … • OK, my first / next / last point is … • If you have any questions or comments, I'd be happy to answer them. • What I'm saying is … • If you look at the poster / handout /…, you'll see … • You see? • In other words, … • This is because … • As you can see on the screen …

Phrases for starting a presentation:

Introducing new ideas:

Referring to media and visuals[1]:

Making a point clear / explaining reasons:

Maintaining[2] the audience's attention:

Finishing a presentation:

portfolio
I can talk, work with words

b) Think of more phrases and add them to your lists.

c) Work in a group and compare your lists.
Try to use the phrases in your presentation.

[1] visuals – *Bildmaterial*; [2] maintain – *aufrechterhalten*

Express yourself **3**

Projects 1–4 ○ Giving feedback

a) What is important to you when your classmates give you feedback after a presentation? Tick your answers and add more points.

When I get feedback after a presentation, it is important to me that …

- [ ] my classmates are polite.
- [ ] my classmates don't criticize me.
- [ ] they tell me what I did well.
- [ ] they give me tips on what I could do better.
- [ ] _____
- [ ] _____
- [ ] _____

b) Listen to some pupils giving a classmate feedback after a presentation. Tick what they say.

CD 1/26

- [ ] your presentation was fun to listen to.
- [ ] your presentation was really funny.
- [ ] you used your notes to speak freely.
- [ ] you looked at your notes all the time.
- [ ] you spoke loudly and clearly.
- [ ] you made eye contact with the audience.
- [ ] you made eye contact with your group.
- [ ] you talked about all the important points.
- [ ] you were able to answer all our questions.
- [ ] you answered only a few of our questions.

portfolio
I can listen

Projects 1–4 ○ After your project

a) Think about the group work for your project: collecting ideas, distributing tasks, finding material, … Then answer the questions.

What do you think went well in your group work?
_____
_____
_____

What did you find difficult?
_____
_____
_____

What do you think should be better in your next group work?
_____
_____
_____

b) Compare your answers in your project group.

E

Exam practice

LISTENING

L1 ● Two jobs

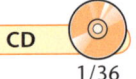

Listen to the telephone dialogues. Tick (✓) the job that the people are talking about.

Scene 1

Scene 2

L2 ● Looking for a job

Listen to the telephone conversation. Mark (✓) the right answer.

1. Linda read about the job …
   - A ☐ in a newspaper.
   - B ☐ on the Internet.
   - C ☐ on a boat tour.
   - D ☐ in a magazine.

2. Linda …
   - A ☐ can't speak English.
   - B ☐ speaks English well.
   - C ☐ speaks English at home.
   - D ☐ only speaks English.

3. Linda …
   - A ☐ has just finished her training.
   - B ☐ worked in Hamburg.
   - C ☐ is looking for a training programme.
   - D ☐ has already worked on a boat.

4. Linda wants to know…
   - A ☐ how many hours she will work a day.
   - B ☐ how many people there will be on the boat.
   - C ☐ where she can stay.
   - D ☐ when the job starts.

5. Mr Miller asks Linda to …
   - A ☐ always be polite.
   - B ☐ call him tomorrow.
   - C ☐ tell him her employer's name.
   - D ☐ spell her last name.

6. Linda is going to send Mr Miller …
   - A ☐ her address and phone number.
   - B ☐ her application and CV.
   - C ☐ her photo and CV.
   - D ☐ her name and phone number.

Tip
Tick, mark and check (= American English) have the same meaning in a test. You may find any of the three words in your final exam.

Exam practice

L3 • Interview with a skydiver

First read the questions below. Then listen to the interview with a skydiver and answer the questions. You can give very short answers.

1. How old is Vicky? _____
2. When was Vicky's first jump? _____
3. Why did Vicky start skydiving? _____
4. How did Vicky feel before her first jump? _____
5. Who did Vicky jump with? _____
6. How did Vicky feel after her first jump? _____
7. How do you become a skydiving teacher? _____
8. How much does each jump cost? _____
9. How much has Vicky spent on skydiving so far? _____
10. What does the interviewer want to do in the future? _____

READING

R1 • At home

Read the e-mail and choose the correct word for each space. Check (✓) A, B or C.

Subject: Feeling better?

Hi Jason,
I heard (0) Nora that you're ill. I guess that's why you weren't in maths class today! When (1) you think you'll be back? Class is so boring without you! Anyway, we did (2) revision for the test we have next week so you didn't miss any new work today. I'm not sure what we're doing (3), but if it's something new, I'll give you my notes when you come back to school. Write back to me when (4) feeling better, I hope it's soon!
Cheers,
Andy

0.	A ☐ about	B ✓ from	C ☐ of
1.	A ☐ are	B ☐ can	C ☐ do
2.	A ☐ some	B ☐ any	C ☐ of
3.	A ☐ yesterday	B ☐ today	C ☐ tomorrow
4.	A ☐ your	B ☐ you	C ☐ you're

R2 ● Different sports

Read the following adverts for different sports. Then match the pictures with the right text. Be careful: there are more pictures than you need.

(A) Enjoy a moment that you will always remember! Together with an experienced "tandem master", jump from about 4,000 metres and fly towards the ground in a free fall! About fifty seconds later, your tandem master pulls the parachute[1] and you'll slowly glide back down to earth. At such heights the ground looks small and you forget everything around you. The seconds in the air will feel like hours. For this experience you should have a maximum body weight of 90 kg and you should be physically fit. Allow at least six hours for this adventure.

(B) Feel like a bird – flying silently from the top of a mountain through the landscape, feeling the wind on your face and feeling free. It's like a dream. And you can experience all this in a weekend. At the beginning of the course you will get a safety and equipment introduction. Then we'll take you to a small practice hill for a few short flights. There you can practise flying and landing. Then you're up in the sky – flying like a bird. This adventure includes a two-day course with theoretical and practical training and all the equipment you need.

(C) Take a day out and experience the excitement of being in the wilderness on rough water. Enjoy fighting the waves in a team. Your success depends on every single member of your paddling team. How much water can you take? Of course, you will be safer than it might seem. Before your ride you'll get all the safety instructions and your equipment. There are qualified team leaders who will guide you between the rocks.

(D) Hold your breath! Move below the water just like a fish. This is the oldest and most original form of this sport. No oxygen[2] tanks are needed – just a deep breath. To take part in this course you need a doctor's certificate and you must be a good swimmer. You will get breathing training and special instructions before "going under".

[1] parachute – *Fallschirm*; [2] oxygen – *Sauerstoff*

R3 ● Read the paper

Read these short articles and adverts that have been taken from different places. Check (✓) the correct statement for each text.

A

Mail - Can you help?
Subject: Can you help?

Hey, I'm planning to go across the US on my bicycle. Will start in L.A. on August 11. I'm ready for the challenge, but a bit short of money, as I'm only a student. Can you support and sponsor me? I promise to update my blog with regular reports and photos from my journey. Your money will help to make a dream come true!

1. ☐ This is an advert for people who would like to go on a cycling tour around the USA.
2. ☐ The author needs money for a trip across the US.
3. ☐ The author needs more training to be fit for the challenge.
4. ☐ The author is planning to write a book about the trip.

B

Complete in-line skating equipment for sale (including helmet, size XL)! Almost new. **Original price $350.** Asking $250 or best offer.
› Quick sale wanted! ‹

1. ☐ This advert offers second-hand in-line skating equipment.
2. ☐ If you want to buy the equipment, you must live in the area.
3. ☐ You have to pay $350 for it.
4. ☐ You can save more than half of the original price.

C

Daniel P. (17) from Basildon, Essex, was taken to hospital yesterday where he is in critical condition. Police say he was hit by a car after he ignored a red light. "In-line skaters using normal roads are becoming a growing problem. They often don't realize that they are putting themselves and other road users at risk," said Police Lieutenant Wilson.

1. ☐ Daniel had an accident in his car.
2. ☐ The police see in-line skaters on roads as a danger to normal traffic.
3. ☐ The hospital is in Basildon, Essex.
4. ☐ Daniel will be OK in a few weeks.

D

Are you a professional model?
Need a new image? Male or female models with medium to long hair needed for the "Young Hairstylist of the Year Award" to be held in London, 11–12 April. Get a free hairstyle and your travel paid for. Apply with photo to the e-mail address below.

1. ☐ Hairstylists are wanted for an event in London.
2. ☐ Models compete for the Young Hairstylist of the Year Award.
3. ☐ You can travel to London for a hairstyle, but you have to be a model.
4. ☐ You will meet famous models at the event.

E

Twenty students from Greenfield High School, Colorado, have entered the Guinness Book of Records. They have just finished a non-stop seven-day table tennis marathon. The maximum break allowed per day was four hours for each player. Only four players were allowed a break at the same time. "It was more tiring than I thought it would be," said Jose Perez, the organizer of the event. "But we are really happy. We're in the book now and what's more important, we raised $20,000 for the local Children's Hospital."

1. ☐ The students won a table tennis marathon.
2. ☐ The marathon took place at a high school.
3. ☐ There always had to be a minimum of 16 students playing.
4. ☐ The event was stopped for four hours each day.

Exam practice

R4 ● Going vegetarian

Read the text and questions below. Mark (✓) the correct answer for each question.

There are a number of reasons why I became a vegetarian. The main reason is because I think factory farming is cruel to animals. Becoming a vegetarian has not been the easiest thing to do, but I'm glad I did it.

At high school, I had several friends who were vegetarians and over time, their reasoning and arguments started making sense to me. I began to lose my taste for meat and ate it less and less. One day, about two years ago, I went to a family party and my meal choices were fish, chicken or beef. I wasn't very excited by any of the choices, but decided to go with the fish. I think I took one bite and after that I could not eat another. That was when I said no to meat forever.

Now I'm a full-time vegetarian – I don't eat meat, chicken, pork or fish. Especially at the start, becoming a vegetarian helped me to make smarter food choices. I began throwing vegetables in all my pasta dishes and started eating a wider variety of foods. What I love about being a vegetarian is that I feel a lot healthier. From time to time I do smell something meaty and I still think it smells good, but I am never really tempted[1] to eat any of it.

I guess the only hard thing about being a vegetarian is going to restaurants and having very few food choices. There have been times when I was out and my meal was simply a collection of side dishes because there were no vegetarian main courses on the menu. I also had to deal with some friends and family questioning my decision to become a vegetarian, but altogether people are very helpful and make changes for me when I eat at their place. I am always very glad about this, but I still feel a bit bad about it because it is extra work in the kitchen for them.

[1] be tempted to do something – *versucht sein, etwas zu tun*

1. When did the writer become a vegetarian?
   - A ☐ After the writer talked to his/her vegetarian friends.
   - B ☐ After the writer went to a family party.
   - C ☐ After the writer learned how to make healthy food choices.
   - D ☐ After the writer visited a restaurant.

2. What is the best thing about going vegetarian according to the writer?
   - A ☐ The writer's friends like him/her more.
   - B ☐ The writer's family makes extra meals for him/her.
   - C ☐ The writer doesn't like factory farming.
   - D ☐ The writer eats more vegetables and feels healthy.

3. What problem does the writer have at restaurants?
   - A ☐ He/she can't find anything he/she likes on the menu.
   - B ☐ He/she has very little to choose from on the menu.
   - C ☐ He/she has to sometimes eat a side order of meat.
   - D ☐ He/she has to ask a friend to bring a vegetarian meal.

4. Why does the writer sometimes feel bad about being a vegetarian?
   - A ☐ Because it sometimes creates more work for people who cook for him/her.
   - B ☐ Because the writer's friends and family ask questions about his/her decision to go vegetarian.
   - C ☐ Because the writer misses the taste of meat sometimes.
   - D ☐ Because the writer ate some fish at a family party.

Exam practice

WRITING

W1 ● The right words

Read the first statement and find one or two words that complete the second statement.

> 0. Parkour is a dangerous sport. You can hurt **yourself** badly if you are not very careful.

1. My friend applied for a work experience placement at a hair salon a week ago. Since then he has been waiting to hear _____ them.

2. A few of my classmates have part-time jobs at the cinema. They usually _____ at weekends.

3. When our school opened twenty years ago, the school cafeteria only served meals with meat or fish. Today, you can _____ vegetarian meals, too.

4. Alain Robert has climbed to the top of many buildings. For that reason he _____ _____ the French Spiderman.

5. Factory farming is all about producing as much as possible, as cheaply as possible. For this reason, animals are given drugs so they_____ get ill nor die.

W2 ● Comment on an extreme sport

You just saw a show about an extreme sport on TV and want to blog about your thoughts to your friends on the web. In your blog post you should talk about:

- the extreme sport you just saw (parkour, kitesurfing, bouldering, …)
- what you found interesting about the sport
- what is dangerous or challenging about the sport
- why you would like to try it in the future or why you would never want to try it

Write 40–50 words on a separate piece of paper.

W3 ● Bad luck

This is a part of an e-mail you received from a friend in the US. Reply to your friend in about 80 words on a separate piece of paper.

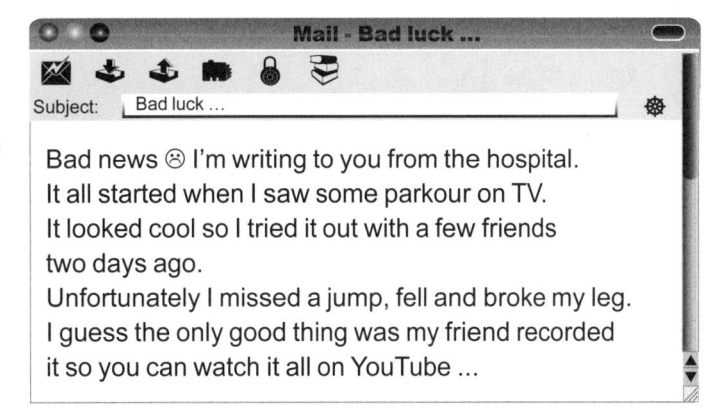

> **Mail - Bad luck ...**
> Subject: Bad luck ...
>
> Bad news ☹ I'm writing to you from the hospital.
> It all started when I saw some parkour on TV.
> It looked cool so I tried it out with a few friends
> two days ago.
> Unfortunately I missed a jump, fell and broke my leg.
> I guess the only good thing was my friend recorded
> it so you can watch it all on YouTube …

E Exam practice

W4 ● Give your opinion or write a story

Choose ONE of the following tasks (a or b). Then write at least 100 words for either a) or b) on a separate piece of paper.

a) **Give your opinion on the topic below:**
   Is it a good idea for pupils to do work experience?

OR

b) **Write a story that starts with this sentence:**
   The first day of my work experience started with a huge problem.

VOCABULARY AND GRAMMAR

Lang 1 ● Sports words

Complete the table about sports.

Activity	What you need (at least two things)
play football	*ball, teammates, equipment*
go swimming	
skating	
play chess	
abseiling	

Lang 2 ● Different meanings

Find the correct German translation for the word "study" in each sentence.

> 0. Our teacher showed us a study on the different places where European teenagers do their work experiences. **1a**

1. Personnel managers have to study each CV carefully to find the right candidate. _____
2. If you have a big exam in a few days, you should study for it each evening. _____
3. It is always a good idea to do your homework in a quiet place like a library or study. _____
4. It is not easy to become a doctor. You have to study for a long time at university. _____

---

study ['stʌdɪ] 1 *n.* a
(= *studying, branch of* ~) (*especially university*) Studium; (*at school*) Lernen; (*of situation, case*) Untersuchung; (*of nature*) Beobachtung
b (= *room*) Arbeits- oder Studierzimmer
2 *vt.* lernen; *nature, stars* beobachten; *author, text* sich befassen mit; (= *research into*) erforschen; (= *examine*) untersuchen
3 *vi.* (*especially school*) lernen; (*university*) **to** ~ **at university** (*to become a teacher, doctor, etc.*) studieren; **to** ~ **for an exam** sich auf eine Prüfung vorbereiten, für eine Prüfung lernen; **to** ~ **under sb** bei jdm studieren

Lang 3 ● Factory farming

Find the right form of the word from the word family at the end of each line. For example, you might have to change an adjective to an adverb or find the plural of a noun.

A lot of people believe that the animals we raise for food live **happily** on farms ~~happy~~

where they live out their days in _____ fields. Sadly, this is very sun

far from reality. Most of these animals live horrible _____ in dark, life

crowded facilities, typically called factory farms.

Factory farming _____ in the 1920s soon after vitamins A and D begin

were discovered. When these vitamins are added to food, animals no

_____ need exercise and sunlight to grow. Unfortunately, mass long

production has _____ in incredible pain and suffering for the result

animals. In the food industry, animals are not thought of as animals at all – they

are machines that _____ food. They live their lives in small cages product

with metal bars and artificial lighting or none whatsoever.

MEDIATION

M1 ● Beyond factory farming

Read this brochure about factory farming. Then work with a partner and tell him or her at least three things about it in German. Take turns.
For example, you can talk about these things:

- what the brochure is about in general
- what you can do
- where you can find more information

Beyond Factory Farming

Support the world-wide movement to reduce and eventually stop factory farming!

Factory farming is all about producing as much as possible, as cheaply as possible.

Here are some things you should do before you buy food:

☑ Avoid industrial production methods.
☑ Know where your food comes from.
☑ Know how your food is produced.
☑ Support local or organic food producers.
☑ Share your food knowledge with others.
☑ Celebrate food and be part of the change!

Beyond Factory Farming
Join the movement by visiting:
www.beyondfactoryfarming.org
and www.eatwellguide.org
Call us free at:
1-877-955-6454

E Exam practice

M2 ● A postcard

Read this postcard with four sayings on the front. Work with a partner and explain to him / her what two of the sayings mean in English. Your partner explains the other two sayings. Take turns.

FREUNDE

Ein Freund ist jemand, der dich mag, obwohl er dich kennt.

Gewinne neue Freunde, aber verliere die alten nicht.

Ein Freund ist jemand, der deine Hand nimmt, aber dein Herz glücklich macht!

Keine Straße ist zu lang mit einem Freund an deiner Seite!

M3 ● Just jump!

Read this brochure about bungee jumping. Then work with a partner and tell him / her three things about the jump in English. Take turns.

1. Interesting facts about the jump
2. Rules for the jump
3. What you should wear
4. What a jump costs
5. When you can jump
6. How to get more information

Bungee Jumping München

Hier sind Sie der springende Punkt.

50 m senkrecht in die Tiefe und dann eintauchen in olympisches Wasser! Erleben Sie Ihren Sprung in der Olympia-Regatta-Anlage bei München – an dem Ort, an dem das Bungee Jumping in Deutschland populär wurde.

Erforderliche körperliche Konstitution und Alter:
- Mindestalter 14 Jahre
- Gewicht zwischen 50 und 120 kg
- Normale physische Gesundheit und Belastbarkeit

Ausrüstung und Kleidung:
- bequeme Kleidung
- Turnschuhe

Kosten:
89,– Euro

Leistung:
50 m Bungee Jump, Urkunde

Veranstaltungsort:
München

Verfügbarkeit / Termine:
Die Anlage hat von Mai bis Oktober an Wochenenden geöffnet.

Kontakt: (0180) 99 99 99 (Mo. bis Fr. 8 – 20 Uhr; Sa. 10 – 16 Uhr)

SPEAKING

S1 ● Ideas for an outdoor class trip

Your English teacher has asked you and a classmate to think of some ideas for an outdoor class trip. Work with a partner and talk about the different things your English class could do outdoors and then decide together what would be best.

S2 ● A job interview

Look at the role cards, choose a role and act out the dialogue with a partner.

Partner A
You are a personnel manager interviewing a candidate for a position as an intern at a large company.

First decide with your partner what kind of job it is (for example, office assistant, car technician, salesperson, cook …). Before you begin, read the points below and prepare to give the interview.

You begin the interview.

- Welcome the job candidate.
- Ask the candidate what his/her reasons were to apply for the job.
- Ask about the qualities that makes him/her the right person for the job.
- Finish the interview and tell the candidate what will happen next.

Partner B
You are at a job interview because you are a candidate for a position as an intern at a large company.

First decide with your partner what kind of job it is (for example, office assistant, car technician, salesperson, cook …). Before you begin, read the points below and prepare for the interview.

Your partner (personnel manager) begins.

- Express your pleasure that you were accepted for an interview.
- Say why you applied for the job.
- Talk about your past job experience and qualities.
- Thank the personnel manager and express hope that he/she will choose you.

S3 ● Two pictures

a) Choose one of the two photos and work with a partner. Describe it as much as you can to your partner. Take turns.

b) Talk together about what is similar in both photos. Then talk about how they are different.

Exam practice: solutions

LISTENING

L1 ● Two jobs

Audioscript:
(Scene 1)
Secretary: Brent Computer World, good morning.
John White: Good morning. My name is John White. There was an advert in the PC World Magazine yesterday and I'd like to …
Secretary: Ah, yes, wait a moment, I'm the secretary. I'll put you through to Mr Brent.
Mr Brent: Hello, how can I help you?
John White: Hello, my name is John White. I read your advert in the PC World. I'd like to ask about the job as a computer salesperson. I'm very interested in computers and I know a lot about …
Mr Brent: Sorry, the job's gone.
John White: Hmm, that's too bad. Err …
Mr Brent: Well, … we are still looking for computer mechanic trainees. If you're interested, I'll put you on my list. All you need to do is send your application form and CV in as soon as possible.
John White: Right, I'll think about it. Thank you very much. Goodbye.
Mr Brent: Goodbye.
(Scene 2)
Secretary: Good afternoon, High Grove Medical Centre. Can I help you?
Kirsty Clark: Ah, yes, good afternoon. My name is Kirsty Clark. Can I speak to Mrs Taylor please? It's about the job as a doctor's assistant.
Secretary: Right, let me see if she's in. … Oh, yes, she is. I'll put you through.
Sandy Taylor: Hello, Sandy Taylor.
Kirsty Clark: Hello. This is Kirsty Clark speaking. I read your advert on the Internet – err – you're looking for a trainee as a doctor's assistant. I'd like to ask if the job is still available?
Sandy Taylor: Yes, it is. We're looking for someone who is flexible and enjoys working with people and in a team. Do you have any experience?
Kirsty Clark: Yes, I do. Last year I did some work experience at a hospital for two weeks. I liked it a lot.
Sandy Taylor: OK, Kirsty. Send in your letter of application and CV and I'll see what I can do for you.
Kirsty Clark: Thanks a lot Mrs Taylor and goodbye.
Sandy Taylor: Goodbye.
Answers: scene 1: picture 3; scene 2: picture 2

L2 ● Looking for a job

Audioscript:
Receptionist: Thames Riverboat Tours. How can I help you?
Linda: Good afternoon, my name is Linda Giebel and I'm phoning about the advert for the waitressing job on the boat. Can I speak to Mr Miller, please?
Receptionist: Hold on. I'll see if he is in his office. Putting you through.
Mr Miller: Hello?
Linda: Hello, this is Linda Giebel speaking. I read your advert for a waitressing job on the Internet and I have a quick question about it.
Mr Miller: Yes, we're still interviewing for the position. We're looking for someone who has worked as a waitress before and … who speaks English.
Linda: I've worked as a waitress for six months at a restaurant here in Hamburg so no problem there I think.
Mr Miller: Good. I can hear that your English is also quite good. Have you worked in an English-speaking country before?
Linda: No, I haven't. But there were a lot of English and American tourists where I worked before. I had to speak English every day.
Mr Miller: That sounds good. You said you had a question.
Linda: Yes, when in June would the job start? My school year doesn't finish until the 15th.
Mr Miller: Our busiest time doesn't begin until early July so that shouldn't be a problem.
Linda: OK, that's great.
Mr Miller: Well, err … I'm sorry, I'm not very familiar with German names. What did you say your surname was? Can you spell it for me, please?
Linda: Yes, sure. It's Giebel, G-I-E-B-E-L.
Mr Miller: I've got that, thanks. Well, Ms Giebel, please send us your application and CV. You can attach everything in an e-mail.
Linda: Yes, I will. Thank you. I will send everything straight away.
Mr Miller: OK, that's good. Goodbye, Ms Giebel.

Linda: Goodbye, Mr Miller.
Answers: 1 – B; 2 – B; 3 – B; 4 – D; 5 – D; 6 – B

L3 ● Interview with a skydiver

Audioscript:
Interviewer: I don't know why someone would want to jump from an aeroplane with nothing more than a big blanket to save their life, but I'm going to talk to someone who has no problem with this. With me in the studio is Vicky Shield, a 20-year-old student studying sports science at Nottingham Trent University. She will soon get her skydiving teacher's certificate. Hi Vicky.
Vicky: Hi Fred.
Interviewer: So Vicky, when was your first jump?
Vicky: My first jump was in May 2006.
Interviewer: And how did you get into skydiving? You don't just wake up one day and go: 'Hmm I fancy jumping out of the sky', do you?
Vicky: You know when you have activities week at school? Well, one of the choices at our school was to go skydiving for MIND – the mental health charity. I was the last person in the world anyone thought would do it so I thought, why not?
Interviewer: So when it comes down to it, you chose to jump out of a plane because you wanted to surprise people?
Vicky: Yes, that's right! You can't believe how surprised my friends and family were when I told them that I was going to go skydiving.
Interviewer: Can you tell us a little bit about the first time you skydived?
Vicky: I went on a tandem jump, that's where you jump attached to your skydiving teacher. I had a short introduction where you find out what's going to happen when you're up in the plane. As the instructor was talking I nodded my head to show I understood and that I wasn't scared, but the truth was that I was extremely scared. It was my first time on a plane as well. The teacher said he'd do a three-second countdown, but he jumped at two seconds. I didn't even have a chance to scream …
Interviewer: That's really funny. So, what else can you say about the jump?
Vicky: Well, I couldn't believe how quiet it was. And the ground doesn't even seem to get closer, I just felt totally weightless and suddenly all my fears turned into a massive buzz, I felt so good.
Interviewer: Until you remember you're flying towards the ground at hundreds of miles an hour…
Vicky: Never even realized that, but then the teacher pulled the parachute. Then we just floated and the landing was really smooth, we glided down and kind of hit the ground running.
Interviewer: How did you feel after the jump?
Vicky: Really excited. I had never had a feeling like that before, I was just so excited to have done it.
Interviewer: OK, so how do you become an instructor?
Vicky: You have to take a test. But that only happens after you've been on many jumps. For example, I've done several tandems, then quite a few on my own and now I'm going to join a formation skydiving team – you know when a team of jumpers forms patterns by holding hands, arms or legs in the air.
Interviewer: That sounds really great. But is it expensive to go skydiving? I've seen ads saying it's 150 pounds a jump.
Vicky: Yeah, 150 pounds is about right. Anyway, it was expensive at first, but when I'm qualified it'll cost a lot less.
Interviewer: So, how much has it cost you up till now?
Vicky: About 3000 pounds, but I'm gonna buy my own parachute etc. in the summer, and that'll cost about 4000 pounds new.
Interviewer: Wow, that's a lot of money. But I guess you don't want to be cheap when it comes to safety. Vicky, thanks so much for the interview.
Vicky: You're welcome; it was my pleasure.
Interviewer: I have to admit that before this interview I couldn't understand how someone could jump out of the sky for fun. I can't imagine myself doing it very often … but after talking to you, I think I'd like to try it at least once. Thanks again, Vicky.
Answers: 1. 20; 2. May 2006; 3. wanted to surprise people / family / friends; 4. scared; 5. her (skydiving) teacher; 6. excited; 7. take a test; 8. about 150 pounds; 9. about 3000 pounds; 10. try skydiving

Lösungen

READING

R1 ● At home
Answers: 1–C; 2–A; 3–C; 4–C

R2 ● Different sports
Answers: Text A: Photo 4; Text B: Photo 2; Text C: Photo 5; Text D: Photo 3

R3 ● Read the paper
Answers: A–2; B–1; C–2; D–3; E–3

R4 ● Going vegetarian
Answers: 1–B; 2–D; 3–B; 4–A

WRITING

W1 ● The right words
Answers: 1. from; 2. work; 3. get / have / buy; 4. is called; 5. neither

W2 ● Comment on an extreme sport
Example answer: I just saw a programme about kitesurfing. It looks fun, and there are many different styles. It must be hard to stay in the air. It's quite dangerous, but I'd like to try it anyway. I can surf, so I'd like to see if I can kitesurf!

W3 ● Bad luck
Example answer: Oh no! I'm so sorry to hear that. Poor you, that must have hurt a lot. How much longer do you have to stay in hospital? Do you think you'll do parkour again? I've never tried it, but now I'm not sure I want to. I haven't watched the video yet, but I'll let you know what I think. Maybe we can talk on the phone when you're back at home? I hope you get well soon! Cheers, Martin

W4 ● Give your opinion or write a story

Example answer a): Yes, I think it is a good idea for pupils to do work experience. It gives them the opportunity to see what it will be like later on in the world of work. It might help a person to decide what they want to do as a career. Or it might help to develop their soft skills, such as being polite, reliable and punctual. Also, it could help them to see why it is a good idea to work hard at school – so that you can get a good job later on! I think doing work experience is something every pupil should do.

Example answer b): The first day of my work experience started with a huge problem. I was working in a clothes shop, and a customer came in to return a pair of trousers that she had bought two weeks before. She said that she had changed her mind about them. But when I looked at them, I could see that she had already worn them, and told her that, unfortunately, she could not return clothes she had already worn. She got very angry and started shouting at me really loudly. I called my manager over, and she politely asked the woman to leave. She did leave, but she was still shouting as she walked out of the shop. It was horrible, but my boss said that I had done the right thing.

VOCABULARY AND GRAMMAR

Lang 1 ● Sports words
Example answer:

Activity	What you need
go swimming	water, swimming pool, bathing clothes
skating	skates, ice, cold weather, arena
play chess	computer, friend, chess board
abseiling	helmet, wall or mountain, gloves, rope

Lang 2 ● Different meanings

Answers: 1 – 2; 2 – 3; 3 – 1b; 4 – 3

Lang 3 ● Factory farming

Answers: 1. sunny; 2. lives; 3. began; 4. longer; 5. resulted; 6. produce

MEDIATION

M1 ● Beyond Factory Farming

Example answer: Partner 1: Es geht in diesem Prospekt um automatisierte Viehhaltung und die weltweite Gegenbewegung.
Partner 2: Das stimmt. Es gibt auch einige Tipps zum Einkaufen von Lebensmitteln. Zum Beispiel sollten wir industrielle Produktionsmethoden vermeiden.
Partner 1: Und wissen, wo unser Essen herkommt und wie es produziert wird.
Partner 2: Wir sollten auch Bio-Produzenten unterstützen und unsere Kenntnisse über Essen mit anderen teilen.
Partner 1: Wir sollten auch versuchen, dass sich etwas ändert.
Partner 2: Entweder im Internet oder bei der kostenlosen Rufnummer kann man mehr Infos einholen.

M2 ● A postcard

Example answer: Partner 1: The first saying means that a friend is someone who likes you although he knows you.
Partner 2: The second one says that you should make new friends, but not lose any old ones.
Partner 1: The third one means that a friend is someone who takes your hand and makes your heart happy.
Partner 2: The last one says that no street is too long if you have a friend by your side.

M3 ● Just jump!

Example answer: Partner 1: An interesting fact about the bungee jump in Munich is that you jump from 50 metres. It's also the place where some Olympic events took place.
Partner 2: You have to be at least 14 years old to jump, be between 50 and 120 kilograms and be fit.
Partner 1: You should wear normal clothes and trainers.
Partner 2: Each bungee jump costs 89 euros.
Partner 1: You can jump from May until October, but only at the weekends.
Partner 2: You can find out more information by calling (0180) 99-99-99 Monday to Friday from 8 am to 8 pm or on Saturday from 10 am to 4 pm.

SPEAKING

S1 ● Ideas for an outdoor class trip

Example answer: Partner 1: Well, we could go to the zoo, I've never been there.
Partner 2: True, but I'm pretty sure lots of people in the class have. Why don't we go to the national park? It's not too far to travel, only about an hour by bus.
Partner 1: Maybe. Or what about that new theme park?
Partner 2: That's a great idea, I'm sure everyone would love to go there.
Partner 1: I don't know – It might be a little expensive.
Partner 2: Oh yeah, that's right. Maybe the national park is the best idea. It's free, and we could take our own lunches and have a picnic.
Partner 1: Yeah, that sounds really fun. Let's see what Mrs Martin thinks of that idea.

S2 ● A job interview

Example answer: Partner A: Hello, Mr Woods, thank you so much for coming today.
Partner B: It's my pleasure, Ms Greene, I'm so happy that you called me for an interview.
Partner A: So, why did you apply for this job?
Partner B: Well, the job description sounded really interesting. Also, a friend of mine did his work experience here, and said that you were a fantastic company to work for.
Partner A: That's good to hear! OK, what qualities do you have that make you the right person for it? Why should I give you the job?
Partner B: Well, I've had some experience working in an office before, when I did my work experience at school. My computer skills are also really good and I am well-organized and reliable.

Partner A: Well, you sound perfect for the job. But I have other people to interview. When I have seen everyone I will give you a call to let you know whether you got the job.
Partner B: That sounds good. Thank you for the interview, Ms Greene. I hope I get the job because I would really like to work for this company.
Partner A: That's nice to hear. Goodbye, Mr Woods.
Partner B: Thanks again and goodbye.

S3 ● Two pictures

Example answer a): *(Volleyball players):* In my picture you can see five people playing beach volleyball. The boy on the right has just hit the ball. I guess the other players on his side are not in the picture. One of them is going to hit the ball across the net. On the other side of the net, the three players are waiting for the ball. In the background you can see a beautiful beach and the ocean. *(Water-skier):* In my picture you can see a water-skier on one ski. He's wearing sunglasses, a black shirt and shorts. You can tell he just turned because the water behind him is to the right and very high.

Example answer b): Partner A: In both pictures people are doing sports. Each of the activities is taking place outside and during the summer.
Partner B: The pictures are also similar because it looks warm in both pictures and you can see water in both of them. The pictures are different because in the one on the left there are a lot of people and on the right there is only one person.
Partner A: They are also different because one of the sports takes place on the beach and the other on the water. Another thing that is different is that there are teams in volleyball. The water-skier doesn't play against anyone.
Partner B: Also, the water-skier is wearing equipment to stay warm. On the other side, some of the volleyball players aren't wearing shirts because they are too warm.

Down under **4**

A1 ● Facts about Australia

a) Look at the pictures and find information about them in A2 in your textbook. Write down descriptions of the pictures.

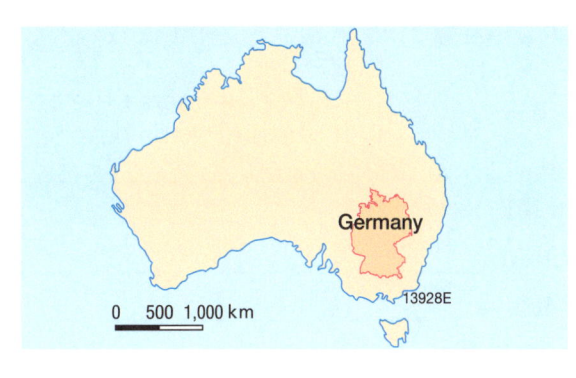

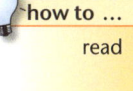

_____
_____
_____

_____
_____
_____

_____
_____
_____

_____
_____
_____

_____
_____
_____

_____
_____
_____

how to …
read

portfolio
I can read

b) Work with a partner. Write eight quiz questions about Australia on pieces of paper. Add the answers on the back.

Then close your textbook and play a quiz game with another pair. If you would like to play again, swap your questions with another group.

59

4 Down under

A2 • What's great about Australia?

a) Listen to seven young people and write down what they like most about Australia. Some of them mention more than one thing and sometimes two people give the same answer.

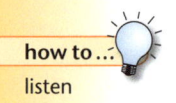

> the hot summers • the people • the mix of people • sports •
> the bush • the beaches • Australian English • the cities

Chen: _____

Malaya: _____

Luke: _____

Tansi: _____

Nathan: _____

Zoe: _____

Fiona: _____

b) Compare your answers with a partner's.

c) What do **you** think is great about Germany? Write a short statement as for an English teen magazine or for a blog.

_____
_____
_____
_____
_____
_____

A3 • Can you remember?

a) Look at A3 in your textbook again. Add questions about Australia's history to the grid.

When …	Where …	What …
did the first people settle in Australia?		

b) Now ask your partner. How much can he or she remember?

4 Down under

A4 ● An Australia comic

Use A3 in your textbook to tell the history of Australia. Write two or three sentences for each picture. Try to use at least two passive forms.

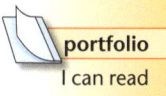

A5 Prisoners from Britain

a) Unscramble the sentences and find out more about the prisoners who were sent to Australia after the new continent had been discovered.

1. were – in the 18th and 19th centuries – Over 165,000 British convicts – to Australia – taken
   _____

2. given – behaved well – Convicts – were – some freedoms – who
   _____

3. allowed to – or to marry – they – For example, – look for work – were
   _____

4. after seven years – set free – usually – Those convicts – were
   _____

5. or return to Britain – could – Then – become settlers in Australia – they
   _____

6. were – who – to special prisons in Tasmania – Convicts – behaved badly – or on another island – sent
   _____

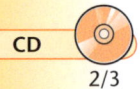

b) Listen to the CD and check your sentences.

A6 The gold rush

a) Most of the people who came to Australia after 1851 to find gold had a very hard life. What made life difficult for the gold diggers[1]? What did they dream of? Add ideas to the lists, using ing-forms.

What was difficult for the gold diggers?

living conditions: *living in tents or small huts,*
_____
_____

work: *working all day without getting paid for it,*
_____
_____

personal reasons: *being far away from family and friends,*
_____
_____

What did they dream of?

getting rich,
_____

Tip
You can use the Internet a or a dictionary for help.

b) ★ One night the gold diggers in the photo talk about their life. Work with a partner and make up a dialogue. Use some ideas from a).

☀ Write a letter for a gold digger to his family back home in Britain. Use some ideas from a).

[1] gold digger – Goldgräber

Down under **4**

A7 ● Five immigrants

a) Listen to A4 in your textbook again. Then answer the questions.

1. Did Lachlan come to Sydney to study music?   _No, he didn't._
2. Does Jan sometimes miss Prague?   _____
3. Does Katie want to return to Korea later?   _____
4. Was Claire born in Germany?   _____
5. Did Hassan leave Casablanca when he was a child?   _____

b) Write down five yes/no questions about the "new" Australians. Then swap your workbooks with a partner. He/she answers your questions, and you answer his/hers.

_____   _____
_____   _____
_____   _____
_____   _____
_____   _____

A8 ○ Aussie phrases

a) Listen to these short dialogues between Australians and read along. Can you understand them?

- G'day mate! – Hi. How are you going?
- Sorry, I'm late. – No worries.
- How was the party last night? – Oh, we had a bonza time!
- What are you going to have for lunch? – I think I'll have a sanger.
- That was some good tucker. – Yeah, there's nothing like a nice barbie.
- Bye! – Bye. See you in the soup.
- Did you know the Jacksons won the lottery? – Blow me down!

b) Read the phrases in British English (BE). Then add the matching phrases from Australian English (AusE) to the list.

BE	AusE
Hello!	
How are you?	
be OK	
barbeque	
Wow, really?	

BE	AusE
No problem.	
a great time	
sandwich	
food	
See you later.	

c) Listen to the CD to check your answers.

A9 Choose

1. Find out the main reasons why Australia is an attractive country for emigrants. Take notes and give a short talk to the class.
2. Do some research on multiculturalism in Australia and why it has a special status. Give a short talk to the class.
3. Talk to someone who is new in Germany. Why did the person move to Germany? What does he or she think about life here? What does he or she expect for the future? Report to the class what you find most interesting. Look at A4 in your textbook for help.
4. Work with a partner. Find out about typical Australian food. Collect some photos, too. Present your results to the class.

A10 Comparing population density

a) If you count the number of people living in one area, you call this number "population density". Use the figures in these lists to draw a bar chart showing population density in different countries.

Country	Number of people per km²
Australia	2.9
China	139
Germany	229
Ghana	100
India	362

Country	Number of people per km²
Netherlands	401
Peru	23
Russia	8.3
South Korea	487
USA	32

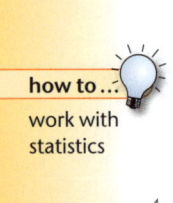

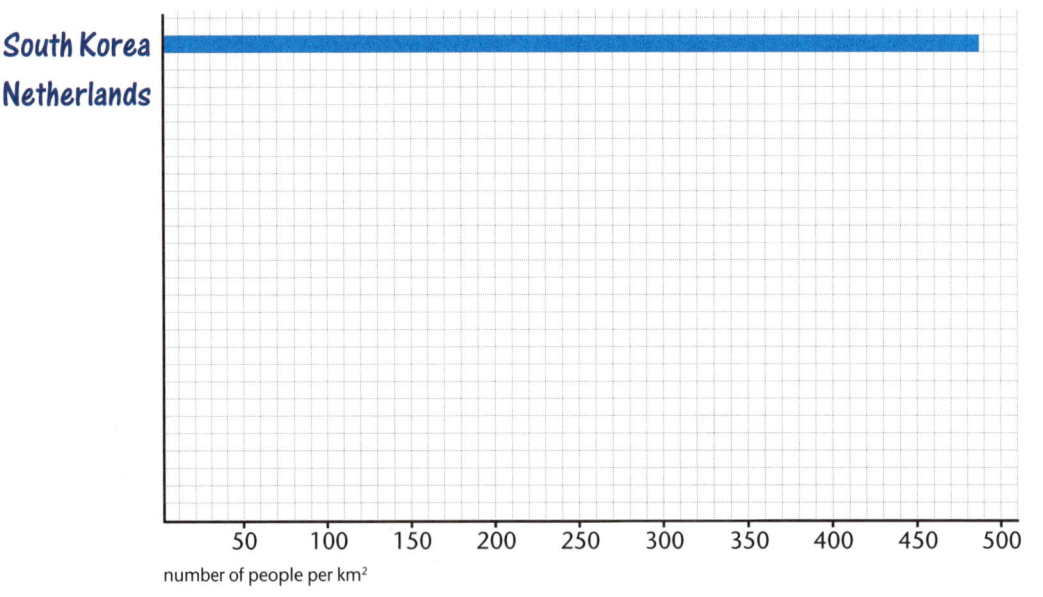

b) Write down some reasons for high and low population density. Compare your ideas in class.

Reasons for high population density: _____

Reasons for low population density: _____

c) Look at your lists from b). Which reasons for high and low population density apply to Australia? Highlight them in your lists. Can you add further ideas to b)?

Choose another continent and do some research on population density there. Find a map. Give a three-minute talk to the class.

Tip: Use the Internet if you are not sure.

A11 ● A trip to Sydney

Your family is going to spend the summer holidays in Australia. One stop will be Sydney. You find this website, but your parents are too busy to sit down at the computer with you and ask you to tell them the most important information in German.

- Tell them what the weather will probably be like.
- Suggest what you could do in Sydney and give reasons.

how to … mediate

portfolio — I can mediate

Sydney, the oldest Australian city, is one of the most fascinating places to visit down under. The fantastic sightseeing, excellent restaurants, great shopping and fun nightlife make Sydney one of the most popular travel destinations in the world.

Weather
Sydney, which is located on Australia's South East coast, has mild winters and warm summers. The warmest month is January, with temperatures between 18° and 25° C, while the coldest month is July, with temperatures between 8° and 15° C. It rains as much in summer as in winter and there is no snow at all.

What to do
Sydney is most famous for its two landmarks: the Opera House and the Harbour Bridge. The Opera House is one of the most recognizable buildings of the modern world. Each year, about 3000 events are held here, while as many as 200,000 travellers tour the building.
If you want to go up on Sydney Harbour Bridge, you can either use a footpath or, if you are an adventure traveller, there is the possibility to climb the southern half of the bridge. On New Year's you can always see fantastic fireworks here.

The Sydney Tower is another attraction. From its roof, 260 metres above the city, visitors have a 360° view of the city.
South of Sydney Harbour, you will find the Royal Botanical Gardens. During spring, when the flowers and trees are in blossom, the gardens look fantastic and are the perfect place to take lovely photos.
For foreign travellers, the holiday in Sydney is usually not complete unless they see some native animals in their natural environment. The Featherdale Wildlife Park is home to 320 Australian species including koalas, kangaroos, birds and reptiles. You can play with the koalas or feed the kangaroos and emus.

Tip: You do not have to understand every single word.

There are also a lot of great museums: the Australian National Maritime Museum, the Art Gallery of New South Wales, the Museum of Contemporary Art and the Yiribana Gallery with Aboriginal and islander art.
One of the best things in Sydney is that you are never more than half an hour away from a beach (except if you stay in the far western suburbs). The shoreline is filled with popular beaches facing the Pacific Ocean, of which the most popular is the famous Bondi Beach.

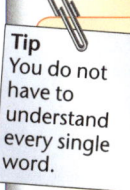

4 Down under

B1 ⭘ Long walk home

a) Watch scenes (00:06:57–00:08:27) and (00:49:04–00:50:18) of *Rabbit-Proof Fence*. Where are Molly, Gracie and Daisy in the scenes, and what do they find out? Take notes.

___

No. 1 Fence (1833 km)
No. 2 Fence (1166 km)
No. 3 Fence (258 km)
Route taken in the film *Rabbit Proof Fence*

b) Now use the map to explain what the girls find out in the two scenes and why this is important for them.

c) ⭐ Collect phrases to describe the girls' walk. Think of the regions they walk through, food, hygiene, … Then tell the class about your ideas.

___

☀ The girls walk 1,500 miles (over 2,400 kilometres). What difficulties and dangers do they have to deal with on the way? How do the girls react to these difficulties and dangers? Make notes and then tell the class about your ideas.

Difficulties / dangers	The girls' reactions

B2 How the water got to the plains

a) Close your eyes and listen to the Dreamtime story.

b) Now you have time to write about the story. You can also draw a picture.

c) What is the message of the story? Do you know a similar story?

B3 Symbols of desert art

a) These symbols are often used in Aboriginal paintings. Look up new words in a dictionary.

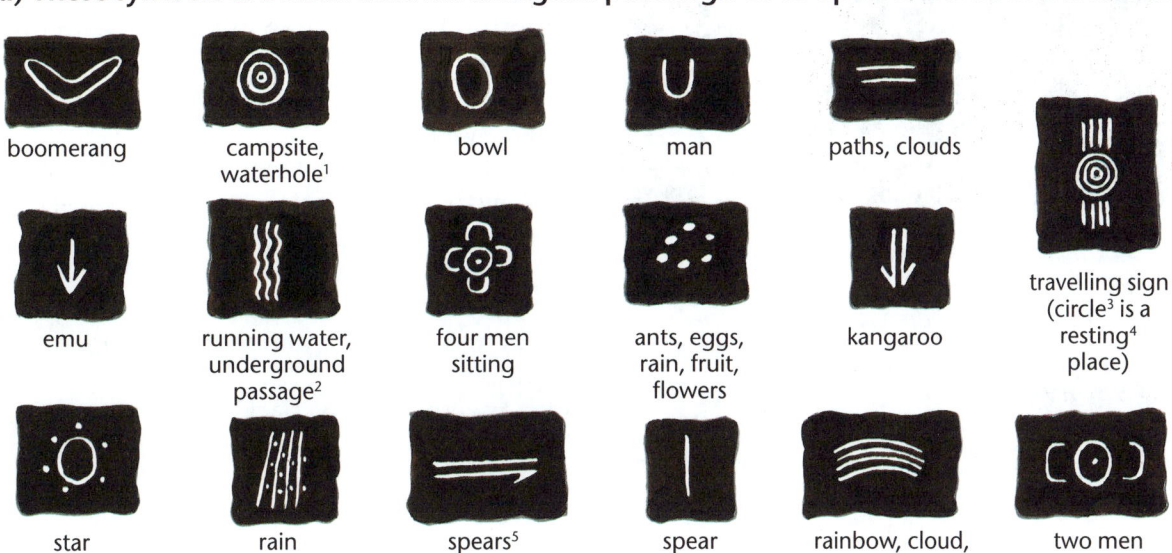

- boomerang
- campsite, waterhole[1]
- bowl
- man
- paths, clouds
- travelling sign (circle[3] is a resting[4] place)
- emu
- running water, underground passage[2]
- four men sitting
- ants, eggs, rain, fruit, flowers
- kangaroo
- star
- rain
- spears[5]
- spear
- rainbow, cloud, cliff[6], sandhill
- two men sitting

[1] waterhole – *Wasserloch*; [2] passage – *Durchgang; Passage*; [3] circle – *Kreis*;
[4] to rest – *(aus)ruhen*; [5] spear – *Speer*; [6] cliff – *Klippe*

b) Work in groups. Look at the painting below and try to find some symbols in it. Describe what the painting might say.

It might mean / express that …

Perhaps it shows that …

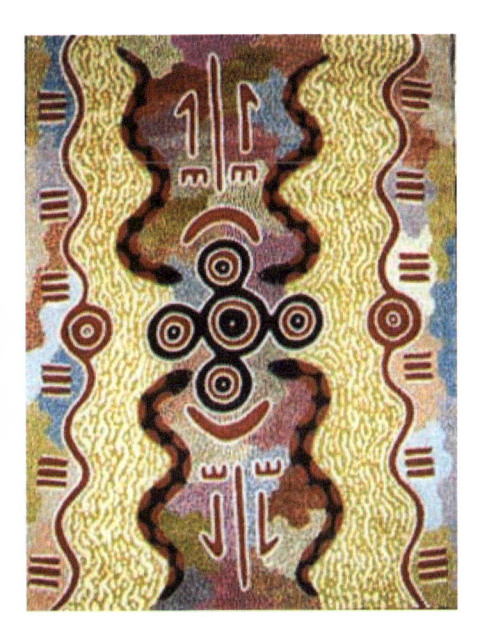

c) Read the Dreamtime story.

Two Kangaroo Dreaming
Michael Nelson Jagamarra, Walpiri, NT

When two kangaroo ancestors sat down to eat they woke up the Rainbow Snakes. The Rainbow Snakes were very angry and tried to kill the kangaroo men with a wild storm. But the kangaroo men hid in a cave until the storm had ended. Whenever they are angry or hungry, the Rainbow Snakes come out of the earth. Rain follows them. When they are happy again, we see their rainbow in the sky. After the rain there is enough food for everyone.

d) Compare your ideas from b) with the story.

☼ Write a description of the painting.

4 Down under

B4 ○ Stolen childhood

a) Before reading: This is a story about an Aboriginal boy who was taken away from his family. What do you expect to find out? Talk to a partner.

b) Reading for gist: Read the text and say in one or two sentences why John told his story.

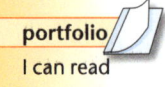

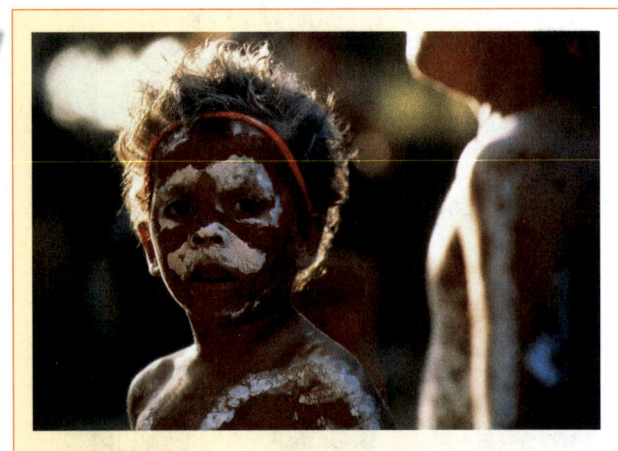

The Australian Human Rights Commission[1] has collected stories by Aborigines who were taken away from their families as children. This is one of them.

John's story

John was taken away from his family as a small child in the 1940s. He spent his first years in Bomaderry Children's Home[2] at Nowra. At the age of 10 he was taken to Kinchela.

We didn't have a clue[3] where we came from. We thought the Sisters were our parents. […] Babies were coming in nearly every day. […] They were just put in the home and it was run by Christian[4] women and all the kids thought it was one big family. We […] thought those women were our mothers.
I was […] not told that I was Aboriginal. What the Sisters told us was that we had to be white. It was drummed into[5] our heads that we were white. It didn't matter what colour you were. We thought we were white. They said you can't talk to any of them coloured people because you're white.

We almost never saw any visitors […]. None of the other kids had visits from their parents. No visits from family. The worst part is, we didn't know we had a family.
When you got to a certain[6] age – like I got to 10 years old […] they just told us we were going on a train trip […] The old man from La Perouse took us […] from Bomaderry to Kinchela Boys' Home. That's when our problems really started – you know!
This is where we learned that we weren't white. […] They took us around to a room and shaved[7] our hair off. […] They gave you your clothes and stamped[8] a number on them. […] They never called you by your name; they called you by your number. That number was stamped on everything. […]
If we answered an adult back[9] we were "sent up the line"[10]. Now I don't know if you can imagine, 79 boys punching[11] the hell out of you […]. Even your brother, your cousin. […] They had to – if they didn't do it, they were sent up the line. […]
Kinchela was a place where they thought you were animals. […]
We never went into town […] the school was in the home […] all we did was work, work, work. Every six months you were dressed up. You got to wear a white shirt. The welfare used to come up […] to see if everything was OK – every six months.
We were prisoners from when we were born. […] Even today they have our file number so we're still prisoners, you know. And we'll always be prisoners while our files are in archives.[12]

---

[1] Human Rights Commission – *Menschenrechtskommission;* [2] home – *Heim;* [3] clue – *Ahnung;* [4] Christian – *christlich;* [5] drum sth into sb – *jdm etwas einhämmern;* [6] certain – *gewiss, bestimmt;* [7] shave – *rasieren;* [8] stamp – *stempeln;* [9] answer back – *widersprechen, freche Antworten geben;* [10] send sb up the line – *hier: jdn. eine Reihe von Personen entlangschicken, die ihn verprügeln;* [11] punch – *mit der Faust schlagen;* [12] archive – *Archiv*

c) Second reading:
- First make a grid like this in your exercise book.

Type of question	Question	Answer	How I found the answer

Tip
Look at pages 13 and 14 in this workbook for help with QAR again.

Down under 4

- Answer these questions, using the QAR strategy. Your QAR cards will be helpful.

1. Did John talk to the commission or did he write down his story? Give reasons for your answer.
2. Who ran Bomaderry, the first home in which John lived as a child, and what were these people called?
3. Why did all the kids who lived in Bomaderry think it was one big family?
4. Why do you think the children were told that they were white?
5. How old was John when he was taken to the second home?
6. What was life at Kinchela Boys' Home like? Find at least five phrases to describe it.
7. Why were the boys dressed very nicely sometimes?
8. Why does John think he has spent his life as a prisoner?
9. How do you think John felt when he heard Kevin Rudd's "sorry speech"? Give reasons for your answer.

- First compare your notes with a partner's, then compare them in class.

d) **After reading:** What did you find most surprising or even shocking when reading John's story? Did you find out what you expected? Talk about your ideas in class.

B5 • Word formation

a) Find a noun for each verb and write the pairs into the right list. Use a dictionary if you aren't sure.

cover • form • introduce • hope • separate • end • isolate • promise • fight • humiliate • discriminate • contact • locate • support

-(a)tion		-no change	
introduce – introduction	separate – separation	cover – cover	

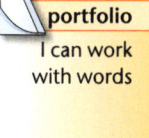

b) Listen to the CD and check your lists.

c) Add more verb-noun pairs to the lists.

B6 • Nouns or adjectives?

a) Use red to mark the nouns in this list. Use yellow to mark the adjectives.

| flowering | painting | surprising | surfing | fascinating |
| dancing | stunning | rewarding | swimming | landing |

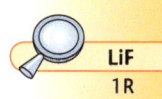

b) Find more nouns and adjectives ending in -ing.

nouns ending in -ing: _____

_____

adjectives ending in -ing: _____

_____

B7 Shannon's life out there

a) Fill in the right prepositions.

1. Shannon lives _____ the Birdsville Track.
2. Life is tough _____ the outback.
3. Out there the water is 700 metres _____ the surface.
4. Shannon will join her brother _____ boarding school _____ Adelaide next year.
5. Her lessons are taught _____ the School of the Air _____ telephone and Internet.
6. After school she sometimes works with the cattle _____ her family's station.
7. Radio contact is vital _____ such a large property as Dulkannina.
8. People _____ the outback are linked _____ the world _____ air routes.
9. For example, the postman, who is called "postie", comes _____ plane once a week.

b) Listen to the CD and check your sentences.

B8 Questions about the outback

a) Some British pupils want to give a presentation on the Australian outback in Geography and have collected ideas for their research. Write down their questions.

Brian would like to know what wildlife you can find in the outback.

Brian: "What wildlife _____

Germaine would like to know what plants grow there.

Germaine: _____

Robert would like to know if there are any national parks in the outback.

_____

Rick would like to know how many cattle are grown on a cattle station.

_____

Janine would like to know what farmers do to keep wild animals away.

_____

b) What would you be interested in if you had to give a talk on the outback? Write down what would you like to know.

I would like to know _____

c) Choose two questions and find the answers on the Internet. Take notes.

d) Compare in class what you found out about the outback.

Down under **4**

B9 ○ At the youth hostel

Shannon's cousin, Dennis, who is 22 and lives in the UK, has decided to visit his relatives during the Christmas holidays. On the way he stops at a youth hostel for one night.

a) Listen to Dennis and the receptionist[1]. Tick the phrases you can hear.

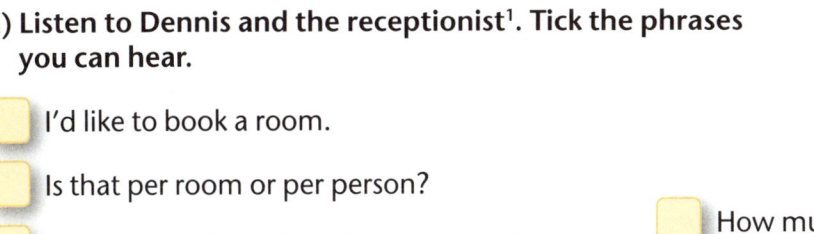

- [ ] I'd like to book a room.
- [ ] Is that per room or per person?
- [ ] We have single and double rooms and mixed dorms[2].
- [ ] How many beds are there in a mixed dorm?
- [ ] Would you like a single or a double room?
- [ ] How much are the double rooms and dorms?
- [ ] How much are the singles?
- [ ] A single room is 30 A$.
- [ ] Is breakfast included?
- [ ] When do I have to pay?
- [ ] I just need your signature here, please.

b) Listen again. Then explain these words:

single room • dorm • 30 A$ • included • signature

c) Work with a partner. Make up a dialogue and act it out. One of you is the receptionist, and the other one is the guest who wants to book a room. Make notes first.

[1] receptionist – *Empfangschef, Empfangsdame*; [2] dorm – *Schlafsaal*

B10 ● Sound check

a) Listen to the CD and repeat the words. How are the sounds marked in red pronounced?

c**oa**st, Ab**o**rigine, A**u**stralia, disc**o**ver, v**o**te, p**o**rt, p**o**pulation, Eur**o**pean
am**o**ng, expl**o**re, gr**o**w, c**o**ntact, supp**o**rt, c**o**mmunity, g**o**vernment

[ɒ]			
[əʊ]			
[ə]			
[ɔː]			
[ʌ]			

b) Write the words into the right list.

c) Listen to the CD and check your lists.

B11 ○ Choose

1. Choose an interesting figure, e.g. the Greek population of Melbourne, and compare it to other places. Make a statistic.

2. Write your own Dreamtime story and illustrate it. Then present it to the class.

3. Talk to a partner. What were the three most interesting facts for you in this Theme? Did you find them interesting because you didn't know anything about the topics before? Or did you have wrong ideas about the topics before you worked with the theme?

4 Detective page

D1 What is it?

1. A large farm in Australia: _____
2. An amount of something that you can use: _____
3. The area at the centre of Australia where not many people live: _____
4. All the people who live in a country: _____
5. A school where pupils live and work: _____
6. The weather in a certain region: _____
7. A person who is a member of a country and has rights there: _____
8. The people who live in an area: _____
9. The city which is the centre of government in a country: _____

D2 Write down words that mean the same.

illness – _____   convict – _____   certain – _____

generate – _____   support – _____   port – _____

D3 Fill in the lists.

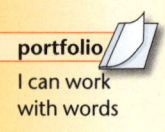

portfolio
I can work with words

noun	adjective
Australia	
north	

noun	adjective
Europe	
east	

noun	adjective
religion	
surprise	

D4 Match the verbs with the phrases. Find as many combinations as possible.

cover • explore • discover • emphasize • create • maintain • connect • grow • send

an order • vehicles • the importance of something • a large area • gold • words • an order • pieces of art • remote areas • vegetables • contact • countries • the countryside • letters • missing things

_____
_____
_____
_____
_____

D5 Good to know …

Australia is home to many dangerous spiders. That's why people should always shake out their shoes before putting them on in case there are spiders hiding in them.

Get connected **5**

A1 ○ Using the Internet

a) What can you do on the Internet? Make a word web.
Use your ideas from A1 in your textbook.

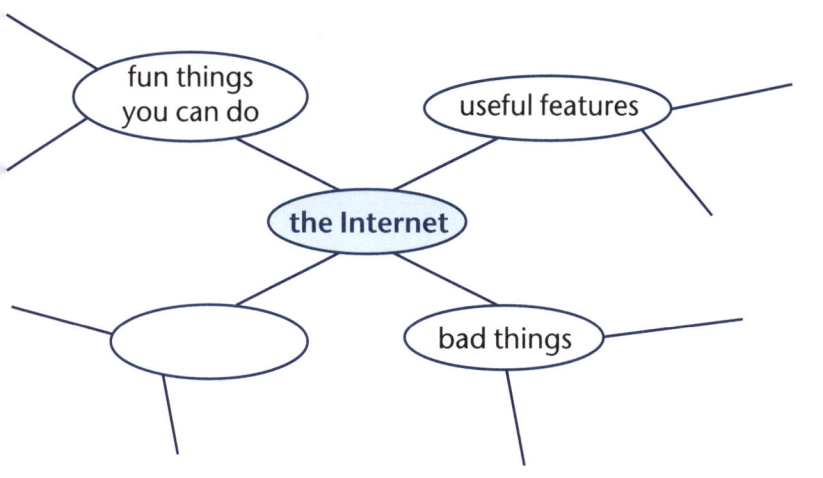

- fun things you can do
- useful features
- the Internet
- bad things

portfolio
I can learn English

b) Write down three things which you use the Internet for.

A2 ● Have you ever …?

a) Add questions to the grid. Then ask two classmates. Try and find out details.

Yes, I have.

No, I haven't.

What kind of …? / How / Why / When … did you …?

Have you ever …	name	yes	no	more info
… found an old friend on a social network?				
… contacted a famous person on a social network?				

LiF
7R, 20R

portfolio
I can work with grammar, learn English

b) Report some interesting facts to the class.

A3 ● Online "friends"

a) Hannah is finally helping her mother in the kitchen where they continue their conversation. What do they say about online friends and real friends? Listen to the conversation and take notes.

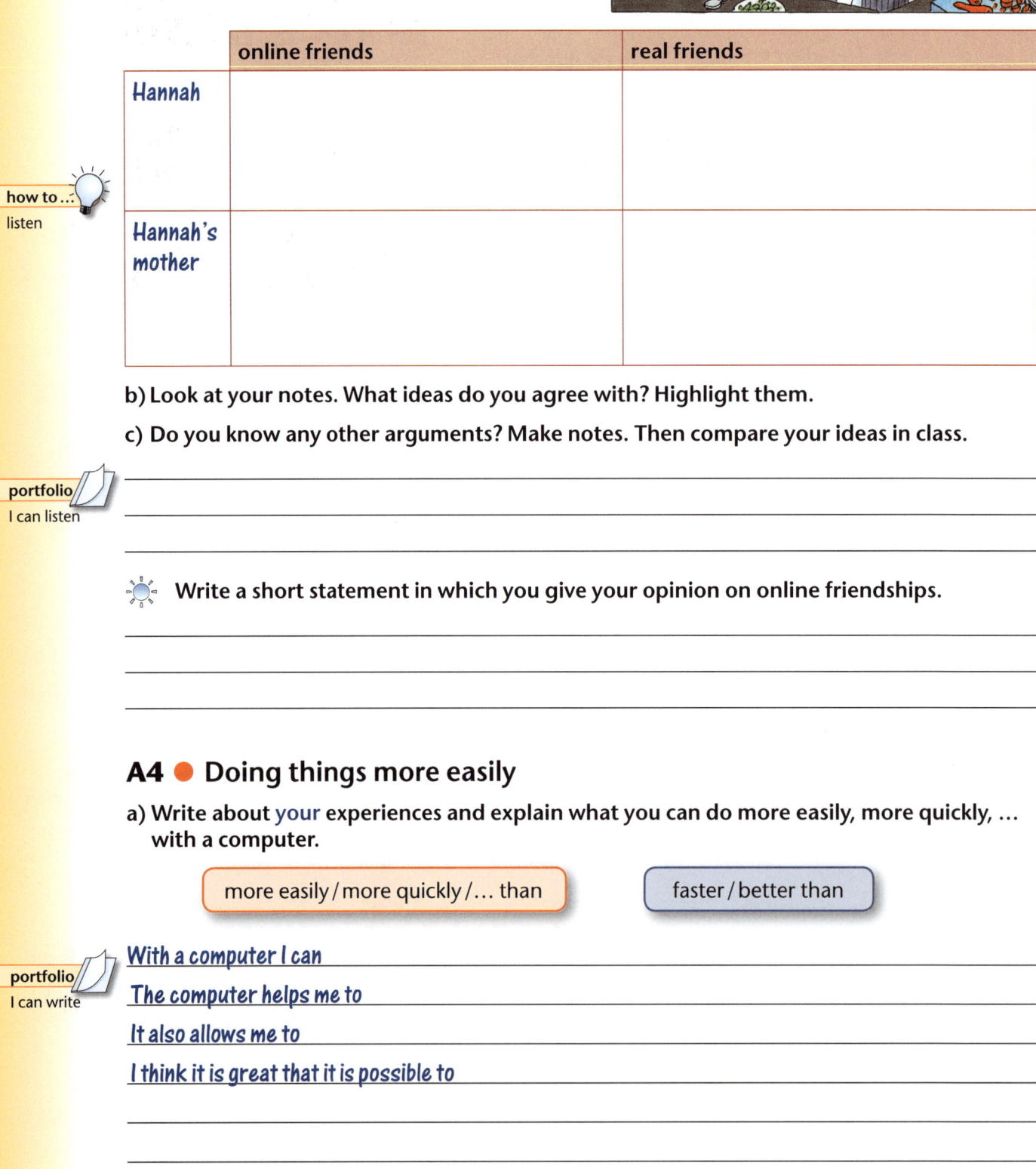

	online friends	real friends
Hannah		
Hannah's mother		

b) Look at your notes. What ideas do you agree with? Highlight them.

c) Do you know any other arguments? Make notes. Then compare your ideas in class.

_____
_____
_____

☀ Write a short statement in which you give your opinion on online friendships.

_____
_____
_____

A4 ● Doing things more easily

a) Write about **your** experiences and explain what you can do more easily, more quickly, … with a computer.

> more easily / more quickly / … than   faster / better than

With a computer I can _____

The computer helps me to _____

It also allows me to _____

I think it is great that it is possible to _____

_____
_____

b) Compare your ideas with a partner's.

Get connected **5**

A5 ● What would you do?

a) Write down what you would do in these situations.

What would you do if …

… your parents told you that you spent too much time on the Internet?

If my parents told me I spent too much time on the Internet, _____

_____

… your parents didn't allow you to use a computer every day?

_____

_____

… you found out that your parents secretly opened your e-mails?

_____

_____

… your parents wanted you to sign a contract with computer rules at home?

_____

_____

b) Compare your ideas in class.

c) Think of other problems between parents and children. Write down questions for a partner. Then ask him / her what he / she would do.

What would you do if _____

_____

_____

LiF 21R

portfolio
I can work with grammar

A6 ○ Word formation

If you add certain syllables to the beginning of words, you can change their meaning. Such syllables are called "prefixes".

a) Add these prefixes to the words in the lists. Use a dictionary if you aren't sure.

un-   in-   mis-   dis-

____friend	____employed	____natural	____dependent	____agree
____advantage	____usual	____guided	____belief	____attractive
____happy	____treat	____dignity	____tolerable	____directly
____like	____ability	____fortunately	____scramble	____afraid

CD 2/15

portfolio
I can work with words

b) Listen to the CD and check your words.

c) Look at your words from a) and tick the right answers.

Which prefixes mean "not" or "the opposite* of"?   ☐ un-   ☐ in-   ☐ mis-   ☐ dis-

Which prefix means "bad" or "wrong"?   ☐ un-   ☐ in-   ☐ mis-   ☐ dis-

*opposite – Gegenteil

A7 • Netiquette

Dos and don'ts on the Internet are called "netiquette". Write down tips you would give the four young chatters. Start your tips with some of these words:

Try to … Always … Never … Do … Don't …

| Samantha writes all her messages really fast and makes quite a few spelling mistakes. | Vera finds chatting really exciting. She often asks new online friends ten questions at a time. | Aaron likes to flirt online. Sometimes he doesn't realize when girls want to be left alone. | Janice easily gets angry if other chatters disagree with her. Then she sometimes uses bad language. |

Why is netiquette important? Write a short statement.

A8 ○ Choose

1. Interview some classmates about chatting on the Internet. Write down four or five questions first. Then record your interviews and make a podcast. If you like, add some music. Present your podcast to the class.

2. Work with a partner. Make a list of the advantages and disadvantages of social networks. Present it to the class.

3. Work in groups of three. Make up a dialogue between a teenager and his/her parents who think their son/daughter spends too much time on social networks. Act out your role play.

A9 • About a computer freak

Read the review and tell an English friend in a few sentences what the novel is about.
Use these words: high-performance computers • artificial intelligence

Add if you would like to read the novel. Say why or why not.

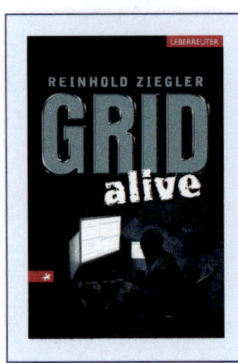

Johannes, genannt Joker, wohnt allein im Gartenhaus. Er ist viel schlauer als seine Mitschüler, einsam und ein Computerfreak. Joker verbringt viel Zeit damit, um im GRID, einem Verbund von Hochleistungsrechnern, heimlich künstliche Intelligenz zu programmieren. Der Anfang klappt wunderbar, weil Joker tatsächlich ein Genie ist, aber er verliert bald die Kontrolle über das künstliche Wesen, das er geschaffen hat. Joker bekommt es mit der Angst zu tun. Zum Glück ist da noch Ljusja, die sich heftig in ihn verliebt und genauso stur ist wie er. Ihr gelingt es, Joker zu klarzumachen, dass man hochintelligent, aber zugleich dumm wie ein Stück Seife sein kann.

5 Get connected

A10 ● Your arguments

"People under 15 should not be allowed to enter social networks on the Internet." Debate.

a) Get together in four groups. Two groups are going to find arguments for the statement, and the other two groups are going to find arguments against it.

b) Work on your own first. Write down two arguments. (They might not be your real opinion!)

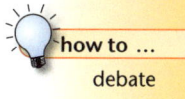

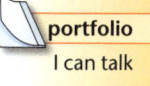

_____
_____

how to … debate

portfolio — I can talk

c) Now compare all your arguments in your group. Decide on the five best arguments and write down the most important arguments first.

1. _____
2. _____
3. _____
4. _____
5. _____

d) Choose two speakers for your group and have your debate.

A11 ○ A word grid

Look at A8 in your textbook again and find words that match these descriptions.

1. First sent across the Atlantic in 1901
2. People who brought news to others
3. The "language" used to create websites
4. 3000 BC people in Egypt wrote on …
5. Invention by Johannes Gutenberg
6. Things you see on a computer are not real but …
7. If you can use a computer without wires you have …
8. A method of sending messages, invened by Samuel Morse
9. A phone with a lot of computer features
10. The first one was sent in 1965.
11. The Internet expanded into the …

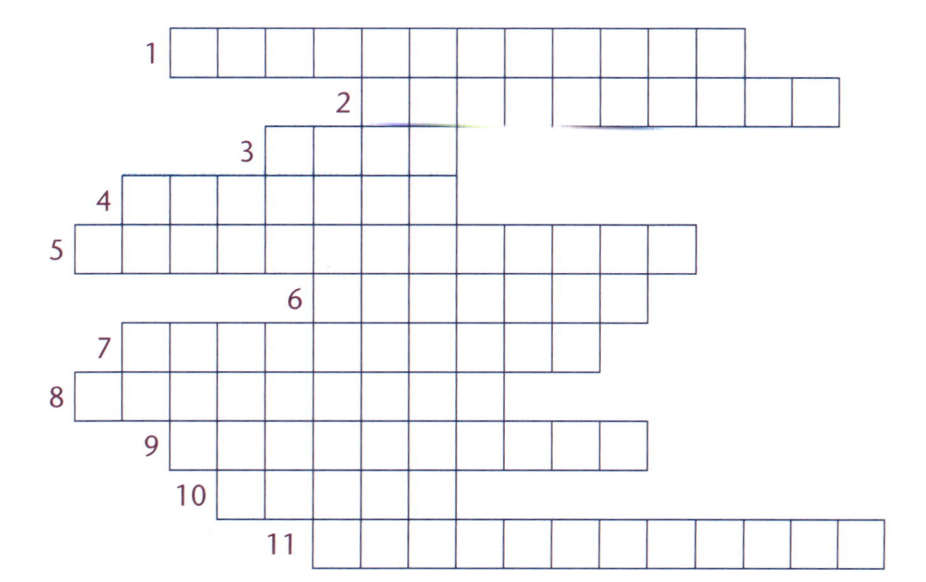

portfolio — I can learn English

5 Get connected

B1 In the PC room

a) Before reading: Have you ever thought that computers have a life of their own? If yes, what happened? Tell the class.

b) Reading for gist: Read the text. Then say in one sentence what is going to happen the next day.

Midnight mischief

It's dark in St Mary's Middle School and very quiet. Lessons ended long ago, and even the cleaners have gone home. Suddenly, there's humming[1] and a strange vibration in the air. In the computer room desktops light up[2] and one by one the PCs come back to life. After a few moments low voices fill the room.
"Hi guys," says Hellhound, the brand new PC by the window. "Everyone all right?"
An unfamiliar[3] voice says sadly, "Hi! I'm Thomas Hall's mobile. He's forgotten to take me home!"
"Never mind[4]," replies Camilla, the PC by the door. "You can help us think up some mischief[5] for tomorrow!"
"Mischief? What mischief?" Already Tom's mobile is sounding much happier.
"Well, we like to cause trouble. We need a bit of fun sometimes! Let's think of some things we can do tomorrow when the class gets in."
"I haven't done the pound thing in a while," says Marvin, the PC with the extra-large screen.
"The pound thing?" Tom's mobile seems confused.
"Yeah, when my pupils touch the £ symbol – bang[6] – I close down the file[7]. Right in the middle of a sentence! And if they haven't saved for a while … well, that's just bad luck."
"I'll do the printer thing," Camilla says. "Every time my pupils hit the printer button, I'll send their file to the headmaster's office. And by the time they notice what's happening, there'll be ten copies[8] of the same stupid text on his desk!"
"Brilliant," says Iron Lady, the PC next to the blackboard. "I'll make sure my pupils can't save a single document without having to give it a new name first. I just love it when they get angry!"

"But be careful," says Boggins, the oldest and most experienced PC in the room. "We mustn't overdo[9] it. If we push them too far, they might call Mr Stephens." Hearing that name, the monitors light up with fear.
"Mr Stephens? Who's Mr Stephens?" asks the mobile.
"Where do you live? Under a rock?" asks Iron Lady.
"No, in Tom's back pocket … when he remembers to take me with him. We can't all live on desks with a nice view of the schoolyard!"
"Well," Camilla says, "at least you get around a bit." And then she adds, in a quiet voice, as if it were dangerous to say the name aloud, "Mr Stephens is the IT guy. You see, the teachers know that most computer problems will sort themselves out[10] after a while."
"When we get bored with causing trouble," Boggins adds.
"But if we go too far," Camilla continues, "they'll call him in. And then, well …"
"Well … What?" asks the mobile.
"He doesn't believe in the idea that we have a life of our own. He can't accept it." Camilla takes a deep breath. "He wipes your hard drive clean[11]!"
The mobile gasps[12] with horror, and the computer room goes dark for a moment as the lights of the monitors fade in shock. Then Hellhound's voice echoes through the room again. "Never mind that now," he says. "Do we still agree that we're going to cause some mischief tomorrow?"
"Yes, we do!" The PCs are sounding happy again. Then the desktops go dark, and the humming stops as suddenly as it began. Looking at the quiet classroom now, you'd think there were peaceful lessons to expect.

---

[1] humming – *Summen, Brummen;* [2] light up – *angehen;* [3] unfamiliar – *unbekannt;* [4] Never mind – *egal;* [5] mischief – *Unfug;* [6] bang – *Peng!;* [7] file – *Datei;* [8] copy – *hier: Ausdruck;* [9] overdo it – *es übertreiben, zu weit gehen;* [10] sort o.s. out – *zur Ruhe kommen;* [11] wipe a hard drive clean – *eine Festplatte löschen;* [12] gasp – *keuchen, tief einatmen*

Get connected **5**

c) **Second reading:**
- First make a grid like this in your exercise book.

Type of question	Question	Answer	How I found the answer

Tip
Look at pages 13 and 14 in this workbook for help with QAR again.

- Answer these questions, using the QAR strategy. Your QAR cards will be helpful.
    1. Where does the scene take place?
    2. What are the computers' names and what else can you find out about them?
    3. Why is there one unfamiliar voice in the room?
    4. Why do the computers like to think up mischief?
    5. What kind of trouble are the different computers planning to cause?
    6. What does Tom Hall's mobile think of the computers' lives as compared to its own life?
    7. How does Camilla see Tom Hall's life?
    8. Who are all the computers afraid of and what is the person's function?
    9. What will happen if the computers go too far?
    10. In what ways could the computers go too far? Write down some examples.
    11. Do you like the story? Give reasons for your opinion.
- First compare your notes with a partner's, then compare them in class.

d) **After reading:** Work in a group of five. The next evening the computers talk about the mischief they caused. Make up a dialogue and act it out.

B2 • Using the web

a) Listen to B2 in your textbook again. What do Emily and Jannik use the Internet for? Take notes.

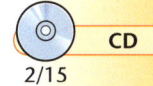

CD 2/15

Name	What he / she uses the Internet for	Your ideas
Emily		
Jannik		
Angelo		
Raphaela		
Logan		
Valerie		

portfolio
I can listen

b) Now listen to four other young people. What do they use the Internet for? Take notes.

CD 2/16

c) Do you agree with the people? Do you use the Internet for the same reasons? If you don't, would you like to try using it for those reasons? Make notes in the right column.

d) Compare your ideas in class.

B3 ● Role cards

Work with a partner and act out the dialogue.

Partner A

1 Frage B, wie oft er / sie das Internet benutzt.

3 Antworte B und erläutere, wofür du das Internet nutzt. Frage dann, wie viele Stunden B pro Woche im Internet verbringt.

5 Antworte und finde heraus, ob B manchmal Probleme mit seinen / ihren Eltern wegen des Internets hat.

7 Antworte. Lade B dann ein, zu dir zu kommen und ein interessantes Online-Spiel mit dir zu spielen.

Partner B

2 Antworte A und erläutere auch, wofür du das Internet nutzt. Frage A dann, ob er / sie dieselben Dinge im Internet macht.

4 Antworte und stelle dieselbe Frage auch A.

6 Antworte und erkläre, warum du Probleme oder keine Probleme deswegen hast. Frage dann A, ob es bei ihm / ihr zu Hause Probleme wegen des Internets gibt.

8 Nimm die Einladung an.

B4 ● What if?

a) Complete these sentences, using the ideas from the box.

> live in the neighbourhood • ~~not live in the outback~~ • not have Internet access • have the chance to play football in the afternoon • not tell them

1. Kevin and Amy would go swimming more often _if they didn't live in the outback._

2. They wouldn't be able to do their project on "Marine life in danger" _if they_ _____

3. The students wouldn't know how to present their results _if Miss Hart_ _____

4. Perhaps Kevin wouldn't like helping on the farm _if he_ _____

5. And Amy would perhaps read fewer books _if more friends_ _____

b) Listen to the CD and check your answers.

Complete these sentences. Look at B3 in your textbook for ideas.

1. Students of the School of the Air would have problems doing research _if they didn't_ _____

2. They would not have as many ideas for their work _if_ _____

3. Perhaps some of them would not understand their teacher's instructions _if_ _____

4. Some of them might feel lonely _if_ _____

Get connected 5

B5 ○ Choose

1. There are some people who still don't use the Internet. Make an information leaflet for them, advertising the advantages of the Internet.

2. Work in a group. Make some fact files about famous people in the computer world (Bill Gates, Steve Jobs, Konrad Zuse, Michael Dell, Sabeer Bhatia, Tim Berners-Lee, …). Add pictures. Then put up your fact files in class.

portfolio
I can combine skills

3. Think of situations when the Internet was really helpful for your school work, for example when you had to give a presentation. Make notes and tell the class.

4. Do you think students should be allowed to use the Internet during exams? Why or why not? Note down some arguments and give a two-minute talk to the class.

B6 ● What did you use to do?

a) What did you use to do when you were younger? Write about things you no longer do now, for example when you were in primary school, when you were twelve, …

used to

play • go to bed • watch • like • hate …

LiF 23

When I was　　　　　　　　**I used to**
_____
_____
_____
_____
_____
_____
_____
_____
_____

b) Ask your partner if he/she used to do the same things when he/she was younger.

Did you also use to hate washing your hair when you were younger?

Yes, I did.

No, I didn't. But I used to hate going to the hairdresser's.

81

B7 ● A video chat

Sven from Hamburg and his e-pal Mark, who lives in the Australian outback, sometimes have video chats. Today Sven's younger sister Melanie also takes part in the chat, but she doesn't understand everything Mark says.

Listen to Sven and Mark talking. Answer Melanie's questions for Sven. There will be pauses on the CD so you can answer immediately.

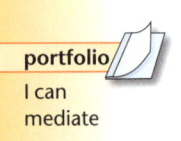

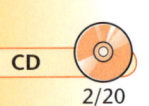

B8 ● Sound check

a) Listen to the CD and repeat the words. How are the sounds marked in green pronounced?

annual	gang	lastly	material	hacking
private	operate	syllable	stranger	advanced
password	aware	debate	broadcast	create
chat	draft	amount	similarity	enable

[eɪ]	[ɑː]	[ə]	[æ]

b) Write the words into the right list.

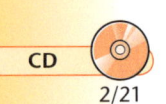

c) Listen to the CD and check your lists.

Detective page 5

D1 ○ Match the verbs with the prepositions.

hold • reply • fill • meet • add • worry • connect • chat • act • get • set • come

out • to • with • up • round • on • about

_____ _____ _____ _____
_____ _____ _____ _____
_____ _____ _____ _____

D2 ○ Use the word list for Theme 5 to complete the verbs. Then add the nouns. What do you notice?

verb	noun
m_ss__e	
r____y	
__b_t_	
d__n____d	
_h_t	
g_ss__	

verb	noun
f_n_t__n	
a___e__	
_o_er	
s____ss	
_t__e	
r__p____	

D3 ○ What can you do online? Match the verbs with the phrases. Find as many combinations as possible.

feedback • lessons • interviews • songs • videos • online dictionaries • online exercises • podcasts • a button • the pronunciation of words • search engines • pictures • software • useful websites • a link • information

search _____   listen to _____
get _____   check _____
find _____   record _____
use _____   download _____
do _____   click on _____
watch _____   bookmark _____

D4 ○ Fill in words that mean the same.

| gang | | answer | | operate | | every year | |

D5 ○ Fill in words that mean the opposite.

| private | | legal | | lastly | | similarity | |

83

6 War and peace

Projects 1–6 ○ Your ideas on war and peace

You have collected ideas on war and peace in class. Choose the most useful ideas for your project work and write them down here.

What is war?

_____
_____
_____
_____
_____
_____

wordbank
war and peace

What is peace?

_____
_____
_____
_____
_____
_____
_____
_____

Projects 1–6 ○ Before you start

a) What do you expect from the project you will be doing in this Theme? Think of team work, results, difficulties, ... Collect ideas in your group and make notes.

_____
_____
_____
_____
_____

b) Compare your ideas in class.

6 War and peace

Project 1 ○ Thoughts on war and peace

a) Make a grid like this in your exercise book and find out more about the people who stated the quotes on page 87 in the textbook.

person	life dates	profession	other info
John Lennon	Born: 9th October, 1940 Died: 8th December, 1980	• musician • peace activist	• member of the *Beatles* • married to Yoko Ono …
Benjamin Franklin			
Herbert Hoover			
James Baldwin			
Mahatma Gandhi			
Martin Luther King Jr.			

b) Now read the portrait of John Lennon and listen to a student presenting it. Look up new words in a dictionary.

CD 2/27

portfolio
I can read, work with words, combine skills

"I'm going to talk about a popular singer, songwriter, and political activist. He was shot and killed in front of his apartment building in New York City on December 8th, 1980. He was only 40. Even though he died before I was born, he is a kind of hero of mine, and of many people. His name is John Lennon.

John Lennon was born in Liverpool on October 9th, 1940, during World War Two. He attended the Liverpool College of Art but later dropped out. He knew he wanted to be a musician, so he started a band with Paul McCartney and George Harrison called the Quarrymen. Later, they became the world famous band, the Beatles. Of course, being a member of the Beatles is the reason that he got famous, but I want to focus more on his peace work than his music career.

So, by 1970, the Beatles had broken up and Lennon and his wife Yoko Ono moved to New York. In 1971, he released the solo album "Imagine". During the US war against Vietnam, Lennon became an anti-war activist. His song "Give Peace a Chance" became the anti-war song. In 1972, Lennon toured the USA to influence young people to vote against both the war and President Richard Nixon. Nixon's government even tried to make him leave the country.

Other examples of his anti-war efforts were the "bed-ins for peace," where John and Yoko stayed in bed covered in white sheets to promote peace. They also wore white bags over their bodies, as a protest against prejudice and stereotypes. And they paid for anti-war billboards all over America.

The news of John's death on 8th of December 1980 shocked the world. Thousands of fans camped outside his building and paid tribute by playing his songs.

John Lennon is my hero for many reasons. He took action against war and racism. His lyrics are meaningful, unlike much of today's music. John Lennon has inspired me to speak up for what I believe in. If he were still alive, I think the world would be a better place."

c) Do you think John Lennon is presented in an interesting way? Why or why not? How would you present him?

6 War and peace

Project 1 ○ The hippie movement

a) Look at the poster and read the texts. What information do you find interesting or surprising? What did you already know? Talk to a partner.

portfolio
I can read, write, combine skills

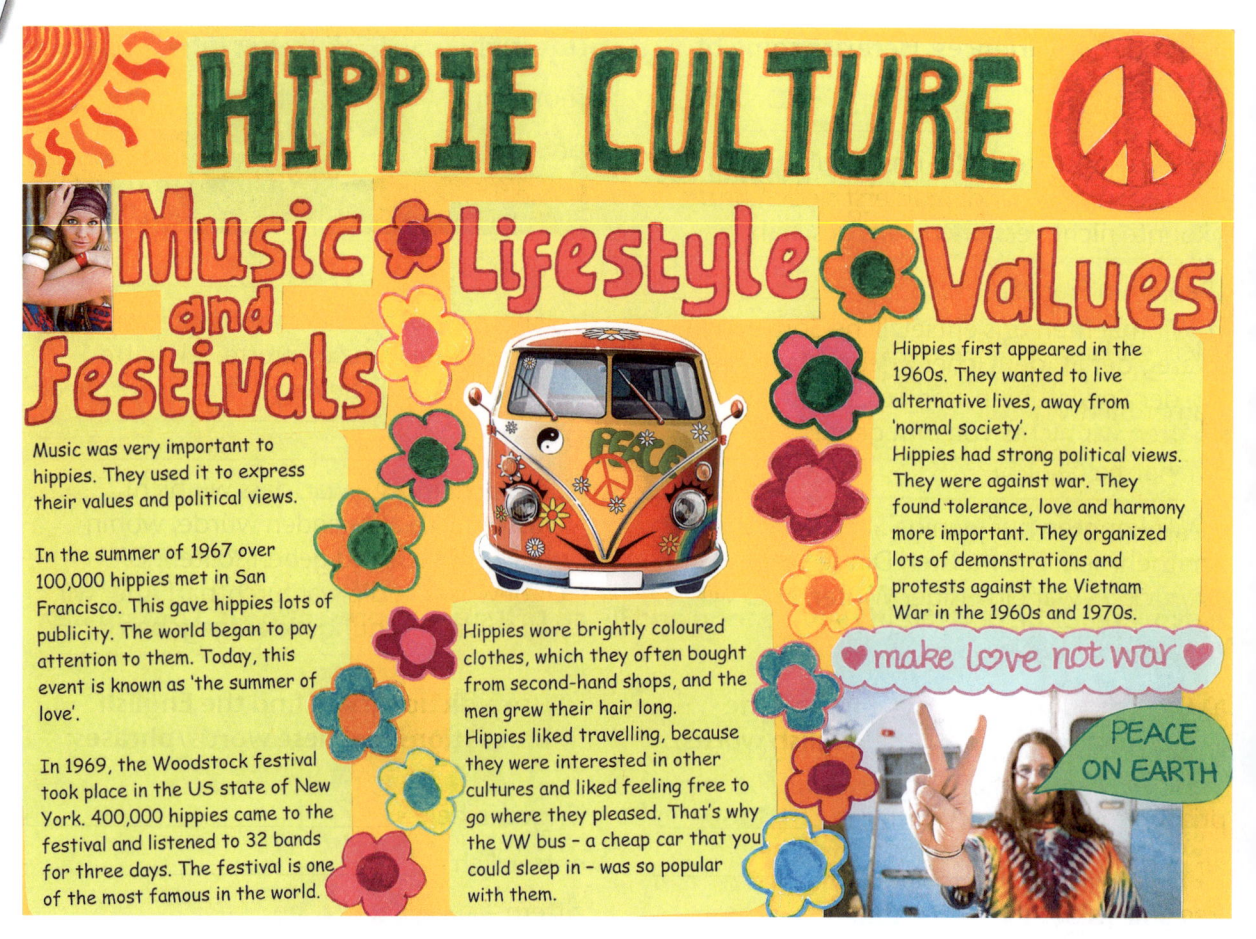

HIPPIE CULTURE

Music and Festivals ✿ Lifestyle ✿ Values

Music was very important to hippies. They used it to express their values and political views.

In the summer of 1967 over 100,000 hippies met in San Francisco. This gave hippies lots of publicity. The world began to pay attention to them. Today, this event is known as 'the summer of love'.

In 1969, the Woodstock festival took place in the US state of New York. 400,000 hippies came to the festival and listened to 32 bands for three days. The festival is one of the most famous in the world.

Hippies wore brightly coloured clothes, which they often bought from second-hand shops, and the men grew their hair long.
Hippies liked travelling, because they were interested in other cultures and liked feeling free to go where they pleased. That's why the VW bus – a cheap car that you could sleep in – was so popular with them.

Hippies first appeared in the 1960s. They wanted to live alternative lives, away from 'normal society'.
Hippies had strong political views. They were against war. They found tolerance, love and harmony more important. They organized lots of demonstrations and protests against the Vietnam War in the 1960s and 1970s.

♥ make love not war ♥

PEACE ON EARTH

b) Now look at the details. Fill in your evaluation in the table and add some comments.

++ really good   + good   – OK   – – needs more work

What do you think of …	evaluation	comments
the layout and the use of colour in the poster?		
the lettering and the size of writing?		
the use of photos and pictures?		
the structure of the poster?		
the information presented on the poster?		

c) Talk in your project group. Compare your ideas about the poster.

d) What would *you* do the same way? What would *you* do differently?

6 War and peace

Project 1 ○ Quoting interviewees

Frau Herrmann, an elderly lady whose family had to flee from Gdansk (formerly called Danzig) in 1945, gave an interview about her experiences. Here are some of her statements.

„Es war so schrecklich, unser Zuhause zu verlassen. Ich war damals erst sieben und konnte nicht verstehen, was geschah."

„Wir machten uns entsetzliche Sorgen um Vater, der als deutscher Kriegsgefangener in der Sowjetunion war. Seit vielen Wochen hatten wir nichts von ihm gehört."

„Wir konnten nur wenige Sachen im Zug mitnehmen. Die meisten Dinge ließen wir zurück. Es war ein eisiger Winter, aber wir hatten kaum Kleidung dabei."

„Ich weiß noch, wie ich bei den Luftangriffen auf Danzig zitterte. Ich hatte immer schreckliche Angst."

„Das Schlimmste war, dass wir nicht wussten, wie alles enden würde, wohin wir in Deutschland gehen sollten. Die Ungewissheit, die war furchtbar! Aber wir haben die Hoffnung nie aufgegeben."

a) Look at the statements and find the German words for these English words/phrases:

prisoner of war – _____

air raid – _____

freezing cold – _____

Soviet Union – _____

Gdansk – _____

b) Use a dictionary to find the English translations for these words/phrases:

Ungewissheit – _____

entsetzlich – _____

zittern – _____

schreckliche Angst haben – _____

portfolio
I can work with words

c) Choose two statements that you would quote in direct speech on a poster or as subtitles in a video. Write down the English versions you would present.

" _____

_____

_____

_____

how to …
mediate

" _____

_____

_____

_____

portfolio
I can mediate

d) Work with a partner. Edit each other's English versions.

6 War and peace

Project 2 ○ Talking about the historical background of events

portfolio
I can read, work with words, combine skills

a) Look at Frau Herrmann's statements on page 87 again. Then read these short texts and look up new words.

b) Read the texts again and find facts that explain the historical background of Frau Herrmann's war memories. Mark key phrases.

> Gdansk is a city on the Baltic coast and Poland's most important seaport. The city, which is situated at the mouth of the Motława River, is connected to the Polish capital Warsaw via a large waterway system.

> In 1919, after World War I, Gdansk became the Free City of Danzig. It was independent in many respects, but Poland had certain rights, such as using the harbour. This led to conflicts between the city and the Polish government.

> In the 1930s, the German government under the Nazi Party wanted Gdansk to become part of Germany, and the German population of Gdansk wanted the same. On September 1, 1939, Germany started World War II by invading Poland. The first German attack was in Gdansk where Polish military positions were bombarded. Shortly afterwards the city became part of Nazi Germany.

> In 1941, Germany started the invasion of the Soviet Union, but the Soviet Army was stronger. In 1944, many Germans who lived in Central and Eastern Europe left their homes and fled to Gdansk where they tried to get on a train or a ship to the West. In late 1944 and early 1945 the city was bombarded heavily. After the final Soviet offensive began in January 1945, hundreds of thousands of German refugees tried to escape through the city's port. The Soviet Army captured Gdansk on March 30, 1945.

c) Work with a partner. Compare the facts you have highlighted. Explain why they are important in order to understand Frau Herrmann's memories.

> I marked the words … because Frau Herrmann talked about … That was probably in …

> I marked the phrases / the date … In 1945 …, which is why Frau Herrmann's family …

d) What would you say about the historical background of Frau Herrmann's war memories? Continue this introduction to a presentation and explain the situation in Gdansk.

Today I'm going to talk about the war memories of an elderly lady living in our neighbourhood. Her name is Agnes Herrmann. She was born in Gdansk in 1938. Let me explain a few facts about the history of Gdansk first. Nowadays it is _____, but

In 1919 Gdansk became _____

e) Work with a partner. Edit each other's introductions.

Project 2 ○ Experiences of war

a) Think of details you could ask someone who has experienced war. Look at pages 88/89 in your textbook and at pages 87/88 in this workbook for ideas. Make notes.

- which war? _____
- living conditions _____
- feelings during bombings and other attacks _____
- _____

portfolio
I can write, combine skills

b) First compare your ideas with a partner's. Then compare them in your project group. Add more ideas to your list and use them in your interview.

Project 3 ○ Anti-war songs

a) Read the texts of the songs "Masters of war", "In the army now" and "Harry Patch" again. Find words or phrases from the songs which match the definitions below.

portfolio
I can work with words

1. being attacked from a hidden position _____
2. a weapon made to explode at a particular time _____
3. a weapon that is shot through the air _____
4. someone who controls a group of people _____
5. part of a gun that is pressed to fire _____
6. a place where a dead person is buried _____
7. a rank in the army _____
8. when a soldier dies _____
9. a box for burying a dead person _____
10. the number of people killed _____
11. to stay alive _____
12. a person who tries to recruit soldiers _____
13. to fire at someone as soon as you see them _____
14. a weapon that is thrown by hand _____

b) Choose more useful words or phrases from the poems and songs and write your own definitions.

c) Read the texts of the songs and poems and listen to the recording. Which do you identify with most? Say why.

6 War and peace

how to...
interpret poetry/lyrics

Project 3 ○ Interpreting songs and poems

a) Read the songs and poems on pages 90–93 in your textbook again. Choose one song or poem to interpret. What can you say about it? Tick the boxes.

The song/poem…	… has a speaker.	… addresses someone.	… is about war experiences.	… is about the reasons of war.	… is about the consequences of war.
	☐	☐	☐	☐	☐

b) These questions and ideas can help you to interpret and present your song or poem.

All the songs and poems:
- What is the key message of the song or poem?
- What stylistic devices are used to stress the message (repetitions, symbols, metaphors, …) ?
- Find words and phrases to describe the tone of the lyrics or the poem.

All the songs:
- What is special about the music (melody, chorus, rhythm, …)? Does it support the lyrics?
- What feelings does the music evoke?

Masters of war
- Who are the "masters of war"? Give examples.
- What do you think of the speaker's attitude?
- Why do you think the song has been covered by many other artists?

Ideas:
- Find out why Bob Dylan wrote the song and what he said about it.
- Make up a discussion between the speaker and different people (e. g. a soldier, a politician, a widow, a priest …).

In the army now
- Summarize the story that is told in the song. Think of who, where, when, what, and why.
- What can you say about the music? Does it support the lyrics?

Ideas:
- Illustrate the song in a picture story.
- Make up a dialogue between some soldiers based on the story.
- Find out about the song's history. Try to explain its popularity.

Imagine
- If you imagine the conditions the speaker describes, what would the world be like?
- Which ideas in the song do you find convincing or even surprising? Are there any ideas you don't agree with?

Ideas:
- Search for cover versions of the song, present them and talk about the differences.
- Write more verses for the song starting with the word "Imagine".

The Charge Of The Light Brigade
- Who are the six hundred, and how does the poet characterize them?
- What do you think was Tennyson's motivation to write the poem?

Ideas:
- Find out important facts about the Charge of the Light Brigade. Use lines from the poem and historical paintings to explain what happened.
- Why do people still read this poem about a battle that took place in 1854?

Harry Patch
- How does the speaker describe his experiences?
- What does he say about the future?

Ideas:
- Find out about the background of the song and Radiohead's motivation to release it.
- Present Harry Patch's biography, e. g. in an illustrated timeline.
- Find articles and TV or radio reports about Harry Patch. Present the most interesting facts.

Project 4 ⚬ Landmines

Look at page 94 of your textbook again. The list of countries that still have problems with landmines is long. Research and complete the list. Then draw the map and mark the affected countries on the map.

portfolio
I can combine skills

List of mine-affected states and other areas (September 2010)

Africa	Americas	Asia-Pacific	Europe	Middle East
Algeria	Argentina*	Afghanistan	Armenia	Iran
Angola	Chile	Cambodia	Azerbaijan	Iraq
Burundi			Bosnia and Herzegovina	
			Croatia	

Argentina and the UK both claim sovereignty over the Falkland Islands/Malvinas, which still contain mined areas.

6 War and peace

Project 4 ○ Children's rights

a) What is necessary for a child to have a good life? Think about babies, small children, school children, your own life … Also look at the text you read in your textbook again (either page 94 or page 95). Add ideas to the list.

<u>having a home</u>
<u>having healthy food</u>
<u>being able to go to school</u>

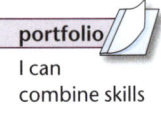

portfolio
I can combine skills

b) First compare your ideas with a partner's, then talk about them in your project group.

- I think every child needs / must have …
- And every child has to be able to …
- It's also very important for all children to have / …

Project 4 ○ Children of war

There are a number of organizations trying to prevent both the recruitment and the use of children as soldiers. Choose one of the following organizations and present their campaigns to the class.

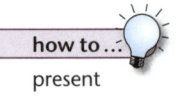

how to …
present

- The Coalition to Stop the Use of Child Soldiers
  (http://www.child-soldiers.org/home)
- Red Hand Day
  (http://www.redhandday.org/)
- UNICEF
  (http://www.unicef.org/emerg/index_childsoldiers.html)
- Child Soldier Relief
  (http://childsoldierrelief.org/)

portfolio
I can present

Project 5 ⊙ War in the media

a) Read the beginning of the following film review and listen to a student presenting it. Then look up new words in a dictionary.

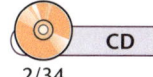

We'd like to talk about the Clint Eastwood film *Flags of our Fathers*, which is more than just a film about war. I'm going to begin by telling you a bit about the plot, and then I will hand you over to Lorna for the next part of our presentation.

So, apart from depicting some of the battles fought between the USA and Japan in the Pacific during World War Two, this film also offers us background information about one of the most famous images of soldiers of the U.S. army during the war.

The picture that you can see right now was taken on 23rd of February 1945 by Joe Rosenthal. In it you can see six soldiers raising the U.S. flag on a mountain on the Japanese island of Iwo Jima.

The film *Flags of our Fathers* starts with the battle on Iwo Jima, but it soon starts to focus on the circumstances surrounding this famous photograph and its content. While three of the soldiers die soon after the picture is taken, the three surviving men, John "Doc" Bradley, played by Ryan Phillippe, Private Rene Gagnon, played by Jesse Bradford and Private Ira Hayes, played by Adam Beach, are taken back to their home country in order to help raise funds for the war. They travel around the United States, giving speeches and trying to get people to buy war bonds.

While the government and the media turn Bradley, Gagnon and Hayes into brave heroes of war, the trio have difficulties dealing with this image constructed by their superiors. Still in shock about the events of the war and the loss of their comrades, they …

---

b) Write down what the film is about.

_____
_____
_____

c) Do you find the beginning of the review interesting? Does it make you want to watch the film yourself? Talk to a partner and give reasons.

d) There are already a lot of films about World War II (1939–1945), but still new ones are still being made. Why do you think people are still interested in that war? Make notes.

_____
_____
_____
_____

e) First compare your ideas with a partner's. Then talk about them in your project group.

6 War and peace

Project 5 ○ Computer war games: exciting or harmful?

a) People have very different opinions about computer war games. Here are some arguments for and against playing them. Write P for "pro" and C for "con" in front of the speech bubbles.

Who could say this?

☐ "Playing aggressive games increases aggressive thoughts, emotions and behaviour. Therefore our campaign calls for much stricter laws."

☐ "I often play war games with my friends, never on my own. These games are exciting and require strategic thinking, so they actually train your brain."

☐ "Young people playing computer games are often isolated and lose touch with reality."

☐ "Our study with 2,000 middle school children has shown that violence in video games does not necessarily cause violent actions."

☐ "Whenever there is a social problem, people say right away that the video games industry is to blame. But it's not that easy. Usually there are several factors."

b) Who do you think made the statements above? Write possible speakers next to each speech bubble. Then compare your ideas with a partner's.

c) Find more pros and cons in your project group.
- First collect all the ideas that come to your mind.
- Then find more arguments on the Internet.
- Also write down which people are pro and which people are con.
- On a poster, make a table like this:

Pros	Who says this?	Cons	Who says this?

Use your table when preparing your discussion or debate. Here are some ideas:

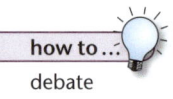

- Do the people in your team have different opinions? Then you can form one pro and one con group. In each group, decide who wants to use which arguments. Practise your discussion and hold it in front of the class.

- When preparing a discussion, you could also distribute roles (e.g. a worried parent, a teen who loves computer war games, a media expert, a teacher, a politician …). Then each of you uses only those arguments that fit his or her role (even if it isn't your real opinion).

- Your discussion could be a role play. You could act out a talkshow on TV and film it, or you could record a discussion in a youth programme on the radio.

- You could hold a debate on the proposition "Computer war games should be banned." Find out about the rules for debates first. Hold your debate in front of the class.

War and peace **6**

Project 6 O Working for peace

a) The *German War Grave Comission, The Cross of Nails* organization and the *West-Eastern Divan* orchestra are just three examples of how you can work for peace. Research other campaigns for peace.

b) First compare your ideas with a partner's, then talk about them in your project group.

portfolio
I can combine skills

c) In your group, compare the different campaigns for peace that you have found.

d) Find words and phrases that describe the effect peace campaigns can have on people.

portfolio
I can work with words

e) Choose one peace campaign. What is special about it?

portfolio
I can write

95

War and peace

Projects 1–6 ○ Collecting ideas

a) Collect ideas for your project. What do you want to do? Make notes.

_____
_____
_____
_____
_____

portfolio — I can talk

b) Compare your ideas in your project group. Agree on the ideas you like best and make a new list.

Ideas for our project:

- _____
- _____
- _____
- _____
- _____
- _____

Projects 1–6 ○ Distributing tasks

portfolio — I can talk

a) Who wants to do what for your project? Fill in the list.

name	task	done?

b) During your project, tick each task that has been done.

6 War and peace

Projects 1–6 ● Giving a presentation

a) Here are some useful tips for presentations. Match the sentence parts and write down the right numbers below.

A When preparing your presentation, consider what your audience knows and doesn't know

B Practise your talk several times

C If you are nervous before your talk,

D Keep eye contact with different people in the audience during your talk,

E Speak loudly and clearly

F If someone asks you a question after your presentation

1 but also look at the whole audience sometimes.

2 and not too fast.

3 so you feel confident when you have to give it.

4 think about it for a moment so you can give an informed answer.

5 close your eyes for a few minutes and breathe slowly in and out.

6 so your talk will be neither boring nor too dificult.

A	B	C	D	E	F

b) Compare your answers with a partner's. Can you give each other further useful tips from your own experience?

Projects 1–6 ○ After your project

a) Think about the group work for your project: collecting ideas, distributing tasks, finding material, … Then answer the questions.

What do you think went well in your group work?
_____
_____
_____

What did you find difficult?
_____
_____
_____

What do you think should be better the next time you do group work?
_____
_____
_____

b) Compare your answers in your project group.

Survival English

1 Being polite when asking for information

It is important to be especially polite when you are speaking English. Remembering to say 'please', 'thank you' and 'you're welcome' is more important than speaking perfect English.

a) One way of being polite is to use indirect questions rather than direct ones. Read the following direct statements, and write down an indirect version of each. Try to find different ways of asking.

1. Where's the nearest post office, please? *Do you think you could tell me* _____
   _____

2. Can you help me with this heavy bag, please? _____
   _____

3. How far is it to the Globe Theatre, please? _____
   _____

4. Can you change a 10 pound note for me, please? _____
   _____

Compare your answers with the example answers on p. 112.

b) Look at the two role cards below. Act out the dialogues with a partner.

Remember: be as polite as possible! Don't forget to greet each other at the beginning of each role play.

①

Partner A: At the station	Partner B: At the station
• Frage, wie teuer eine Fahrkarte nach London ist. • Sage, dass du die letzte Durchsage nicht verstanden hast. • Bedanke und verabschiede dich.	• Nenne den Preis der Fahrkarte. Sie kostet 20 Pfund. • Erkläre die Durchsage: unbeaufsichtiges Gepäck wird entfernt. • Verabschiede dich.

②

Partner A: At the tourist information office	Partner B: At the tourist information office
• Frage, ob die Geschäfte sonntags geöffnet haben. • Frage, wo es einen Club gibt und wie er heißt. • Bedanke und verabschiede dich.	• Antworte, ja die meisten hätten geöffnet, jedoch nur von 10 bis 16 Uhr. • Antworte, am Hauptbahnhof gäbe es einen Club namens „Arena". • Verabschiede dich.

Survival English

c) With your partner, make up two dialogues of your own, one at a newsagent's and one at a museum. Each of you should speak at least three times in each dialogue.

If you need some help, look at these phrases:

- Would you mind telling me …
- Excuse me, please, may I ask you …
- I wonder whether you could …

- I don't mind at all.
- You're welcome.
- You could …

Compare your dialogues from b) and c) with the examples on p. 112.

2 Asking and explaining the way

If you are on holiday in a country where people don't speak German, you may have to ask someone the way in English. Or a tourist in your city may ask you for directions.

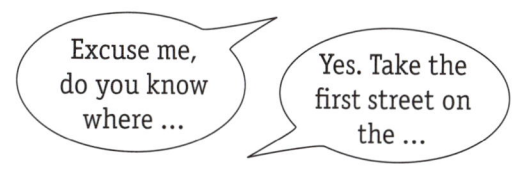

Excuse me, do you know where …

Yes. Take the first street on the …

a) Look at the role cards. Act out the dialogue with a partner.

Partner A
- Frage, wo die Deutsche Botschaft[1] ist.
- Frage, wie weit entfernt das ist.
- Bedanke dich.

Partner B
- Antworte, dass sie in der Nähe vom Dom ist, in der Priory Road 61.
- Antworte, dass sie nur zehn Minuten zu Fuß entfernt ist.
- Sage, 'gern geschehen'.

Compare your dialogue with the example on p.112.

b) What do the phrases mean? Write them down in German. You can use a dictionary.

1. I'm lost. _____

2. Go left at the traffic lights. _____

3. What's the best way of getting to …? _____

4. Follow the signs to the city. _____

5. Excuse me. I don't come from here. Would you be able to …? _____

Check your answers on p.

c) Work with a partner. Write a dialogue of your own, using some of the phrases from b). Practise it and present it to the class.

If you need some help, look at these phrases:

Excuse me, is there a … near here? • How do I get to …? • Excuse me, I'm looking for … • Walk along … • Cross … • Take the first / second … on your left / right into … • It's only … minutes away on foot / by car. • You'll see … on the left / right. • …

[1] embassy– Botschaft

99

Survival English

3 Getting to know people

Imagine that you have been invited to a dinner party at a friend's house. You are sat next to someone you don't know.

a) What could you say to start a conversation? Write down your ideas. Check on p. 112 for more ideas.

_____

_____

_____

_____

b) So, now that you've started a conversation, you need some topics to talk about! You need to be able to answer and ask questions.
Look at the table below. Write down three more questions and then answer them.

Questions	Answers
What do you like to do in your free time?	I like playing football and watching DVDs. I go to the cinema alot, too.

Compare your ideas with those on page 112.

c) Now stand up and walk around the classroom. Find different people to talk to. Imagine you don't know them. Begin a conversation with a phrase from a). Ask them questions from b) and the questions from 3b) on p. 112 to get to know them. Answer any questions they ask you.

d) You are going on an exchange with your school. You will spend a week living with a British family. Write a letter to your exchange partner. Tell him/her about yourself, and ask about them, too. You can use the ideas from b) and c) to help you. Write at least 10 sentences.

Compare your work with the example letter on p. 112/113.

Survival English

4 Talking about feelings

a) **Work with a partner. Read the following statements. Take it in turns to tell your partner in English how you feel.**

Du hast Angst vor Spinnen. **I'm afraid of spiders.**

1. Du freust dich, jemanden zu treffen.
2. Du bist glücklich über das Geschenk.
3. Du bist erleichtert, dass nicht Schlimmes passiert ist.
4. Du fühlst dich schlecht / krank.
5. Du bist enttäuscht, dass deine Lieblingsband nicht mehr live auftritt.
6. Du ärgerst dich über deine Geschwister.

Check your answers on p. 113.

b) **Choose one of the following situations and write a diary entry. Use lots of adjectives to describe your feelings.**

1. You had a terrible day. You failed an exam and argued with your best friend.
2. You had a great day. You spent the morning with your best friend and then found out that your family is going on holiday to Australia in the summer.

Dear Diary _____

_____
_____
_____
_____
_____
_____
_____

Compare your work with the examples on p. 113.

c) **Think of two feelings. Describe them, starting with the phrase: 'You might feel like this when / if ...'.**

You might feel like this when something goes wrong and you think people are laughing at you.

(embarassed)

1. _____
_____
2. _____
_____

d) **Work in groups of four. Read your descriptions to your group. They have to work out which feeling you are talking about.**

If you need help, look at these adjectives:

> satisfied • foolish • better • happy • sad • glad •
> disappointed • thankful • amused • angry • hurt •
> great • lonely • embarrassed • proud • relieved •
> shocked • stupid • ashamed • unhappy •
> nervous • scared • excited • ...

Survival English

5 Writing letters and e-mails

There are many situations where you might need to write to someone in English. You can write formally or informally.

a) Read the following phrases. Are they from formal or informal letters? Write F (formal) or I (informal) next to each one. Check your answers on p. 113.

b) Then write under each formal phrase how you could say it informally and under each informal one how you could say it formally. Check your answers on p. 113.

1. I wonder whether it would be possible for you to let me know ... ☐

___

2. I can't come on Tuesday. ☐

___

3. Can you send me your ...? ☐

___

4. Thank you ever so much for your reply. ☐

___

c) Choose one of the following situations and write a formal letter.

1. You didn't receive the poster you ordered online.
2. You are writing a letter of application. The job is advertised as starting in June, but you wouldn't be able to start until July.

d) Choose one of the following situations and write an informal e-mail.

1. Your English penfriend has been complaining that you haven't written to him/her for ages. That isn't true.
2. Your cousin from Australia is flying to Germany next week to visit you. You need to know his/her arrival details.

Compare your e-mail and letter with the examples on p.113.
If you need some help, look at these phrases:

Formal writing
Dear Sir / Madam ... Yours faithfully, ... • Dear Mr / Mrs X ... Yours sincerely, ... • I am writing to ask about ... • I would be grateful if you could ... • Thank you for your reply ... • Unfortunately, I am unable to ... • Many thanks in advance. • I look forward to ... • ...

Informal writing
Thanks for your ... • Please can you let me know ... • Please would you send me ... • I'm sorry, but I can't ... • Thanks for answering my ... • Best wishes. • ...

Other useful letter and e-mail phrases
Please find my CV / ... enclosed. • I have attached my CV / ... to this e-mail. • ...

Survival English

6 Disagreeing with people

What do you say if you don't agree with someone?

a) What would you say in these situations? Read each statement and write down how you could disagree with it. Think about how polite you need to be in each situation.

1. "Here's your change – $2.50." (You were expecting $4.50.) _____
_____

2. "Arsenal is the best football club in the world." _____
_____

3. "I think we should go to the cinema tonight." _____
_____

4. "A project on World War II is not that important." _____
_____

5. "Why didn't you reply to my text?" (You did.) _____
_____

Compare your answers with the answers on p. 113.

b) Work with a partner. You are going to have a debate. The topic is:

"Couples should not be allowed to kiss in public."

Decide who is A and B. Think of four arguments each, then have a debate.

Partner A
You agree with this statement.
Find arguments in favour of it.

- _____
- _____
- _____
- _____

Partner B
You disagree with this statement.
Find arguments against it.

- _____
- _____
- _____
- _____

If you need some help, look at these phrases:

> Sorry, I can't agree with you because … • I just don't believe that … • Actually, I think … •
> That's not true, because … • If you ask me, that's …

Survival English

7 Buying shoes and clothes

Shoe and clothes sizes are different in America and Britain. Look at the tables below.

Womens' shirts and dresses					
American	XS	S	M	L	XL
British	8	10	12	14	16
Continental	32/34	36/38	40/42	44/46	48/50

Mens' shirts					
American/British	S	M	L	XL	XXL
Continental	44/46	48/38	50/52	54/56	60/62

Womens' shoes					
American	6½	7½	8½	9½	10½
British	4	5	6	7	8
Continental	37	38	39	40	41

Mens' shoes					
American	8½	9½	10½	11½	12½	12½
British	8	9	10	11	12	13
Continental	42	43	44	45	44	47

Womens' trousers						
American/British	26	28	29	31	33	34
Continental		34	36	38	40	42	44

Mens' trousers							
American/British	30	32	33	34	36	38	40	42
Continental		44	46	48	50	52	54	56	58

a) Work in groups of three. Make up a dialogue set in a shop either in Britain or America. Use information from the tables.

Partner A: You are looking for something to wear to a party.

Partner B: You are helping your friend (Partner A) to find something to wear.

Partner C: You are a shop assistant.

If you need some help, look at the phrases in the boxes at the bottom of the page.

b) Work with a partner. Look at the boxes below. Talk about where and when people would use these phrases. Do you understand them all? Use a dictionary for help.

- I've changed my mind.
- Can I ask why you're returning it?
- Can I help you?
- I'd like to exchange this / these for …
- Could I have my money back, please?
- I'd like to return this / these.
- It's too big / too small / broken.

c) Work with a partner. Using the ideas from b), make up a short dialogue in a shop. One of you is a customer who wants to return an item of clothing, the other is a shop assistant.

A: Excuse me, please can I try this / these on? • Where are the changing rooms, please? • Do you have this / these in size …? • How does it / do they look? • …

B: I think it looks … on you! • It really suits you! • Maybe you should try … instead / too. • …

C: Shall I get you a size …? • How are you getting on? • The changing rooms are … • …

Survival English

8 Measurements and numbers

Not all countries use the same measurements as Germany. Nor do they all use the same method for telling the time or saying the date. This can be confusing when you are abroad.

Britain	Germany
1 mile	ca. 1,6 km
1 stone	ca. 6,5 kg
1 pound	ca. 450 g
1 ounce	ca. 30 g
1 pint	ca. 0,47 l

a) Translate the following sentences into British English.

1. Er wohnt 3,2 km von seiner Schule entfernt. _____

2. Du brauchst 90 g Zucker für das Rezept. _____

3. Sie wiegt 65 kg. _____

There are different ways of saying the time and date in English. In British and American English they are said differently. Look at the following tables.

Telling the time	British English	American English
10.15	quarter past ten	quarter after / a quarter after ten
10.30	half past / half ten	half past ten
10.45	quarter to eleven	a quarter of / to / 'til ten

Dates	British English	American English
06/04/05	= the 6th of April 2005 = April the 6th 2005	= June 4th 2005
the day the Twin Towers fell	= September the 11th	= 9/11

b) Listen and write down in German the times and dates that you hear.

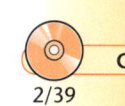

1. _____ 4. _____

2. _____ 5. _____

3. _____ 6. _____

Check your answers to a) and b) on p.114.

c) Work with a partner. Take it in turns to read the following numbers out loud.

> 15 • 50 • 150 • 1.355 • 1922 • 25,000 • 100 per cent • 33.3 per cent • 1/2 • 1/3 • 3/4

d) Now listen to the CD and check your numbers.

e) Work with a partner. Each of you write down three numbers – don't make them too short or easy! Then say them to your partner, who has to write them down. Check to see if you both got them right.

Your numbers: 1. _____ 2. _____ 3. _____

Their numbers: 1. _____ 2. _____ 3. _____

Survival English

9 Buying and ordering food

When you are abroad, you often need to order or buy food and drinks in English.

a) Listen to the following dialogue. Fill in the missing words.

- Good morning, I'd like five white rolls, please.

- Certainly. Is there _____ else?

- Yes. I'd also like two _____ of cake – what _____ do you have?

- Well, today's _____ are chocolate, coffee and cheesecake. Personally I'd _____ the cheesecake!

- Then I'll have two pieces of cheesecake, please.

- OK ... that _____ to six pounds, then, please.

- Great. Here _____. Bye!

- Goodbye!

Check your answers on p. 114.

b) Work with a partner. Using some of the phrases from a), write your own dialogue. It could be in a restaurant, a bakery, etc. Practise it, then act it out in class.

c) With your partner, look at the phrases in the boxes below. When and where would you use them? Do you understand them all? Use a dictionary if you need help.

| Let me talk to the chef / the manager. | Sorry, this isn't what I ordered! | I'm ever so sorry. |

| I'm sorry, but this tastes ... | I think you've made a mistake. | I'd just like the bill, please. |

d) Think of two more phrases you could use in a similar situation, one as a customer, one as a waiter / waitress. Write them into the empty boxes.

e) Work with a partner. Write a dialogue between a customer and a waiter / waitress, using the phrases from c) and d).

If you need some help, you could begin with one of the following phrases:

Customer: 'I just can't eat this. I'm going to complain!'
Customer: 'Excuse me? I'm not very happy, because ...'
Waiter / waitress: 'Is everything OK with your meal, sir / madam?'

Survival English

10 Understanding spoken announcements

When you are out and about, you often hear spoken announcements – in stations, airports and shops, for example. If you are somewhere loud it can be difficult to hear all the information, so it is important to practise listening to them.

Listen to the announcements. In German, write down the main information.

CD
2/42

1. _____
   _____
   _____

2. _____
   _____
   _____

3. _____
   _____

4. _____

5. _____
   _____

6. _____
   _____

7. _____
   _____

Check your answers on p. 114/115.

The language of announcements

Announcements often contain instructions and orders. The imperative is normally used for this.

"Have your passport and boarding card ready."
"Keep your belongings with you at all times."
"Don't forget our designer T-shirt offer!"

Survival English

11 On the phone

There are many different situations where you may have to use English on the phone.

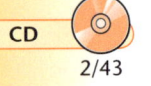

a) Understanding information on the phone can be hard, especially numbers and letters. Listen and write down the phone numbers and names that you hear.

1. _____
2. _____
3. _____
4. _____
5. _____
6. _____

Check your answers on p.115.

b) You need to be able to give information, too. Work with a partner. Write down three phone numbers and three names. Say / spell them to your partner. Your partner must write down what he or she hears. Now check: do you have the same numbers and names written down? Change roles.

c) Just like you can write formal and informal letters and e-mails, you can also have formal and informal phone conversations. Look at the phrases. Decide which are formal and which are informal. Write them into the table. Check your answers on p. 115.

- Would the 6th of January suit you?
- Can you give me your phone number again?
- Would you mind telling me your address, please?
- See you later!
- What do you reckon?

Formal	Informal
Good morning, please could I speak to ...?	Oh, hi, is that Claire?

d) Work with a partner. Write a short dialogue between two friends. You want to meet up at the weekend. Talk about what you want to do and where and when you will meet. Think about what sort of language you need to use. Practise it, and then perform it to the class.

e) Imagine that you spent a year in England. On the next page are some situations that you might find yourself in there. Act out the dialogues with a partner. Think about what sort of language you need to use.

Survival English

A wrong number

1

Partner A (Read the text. You start)
- Hello, could I speak to Jake please?
- This is Rob Brown, I'd like to speak to Jake, please.
- Oh, isn't that 01647 646360?
- Sure, it's 01647 646360, in Okehampton.
- Sorry, I must have the wrong number. Sorry to trouble you. Goodbye.

Partner B
- Du fragst, wie der Anrufer heißt.
- Du sagst, dass er die falsche Nummer gewählt hat, nennst deinen Namen und sagst, dass dort kein Jake wohnt.
- Du bittest den Anrufer, die Nummer zu wiederholen.
- Es ist deine Nummer, aber dort wohnt kein Jake.
- Du verabschiedest dich höflich.

Ordering pizza

2

Partner A (Read the text. You start)
- Good evening, Angelo's Pizzas.
- OK, what would you like?
- Right ... OK, I've got that. Anything else?
- Um, it should be ready in about 20 minutes. What's your address?
- And your phone number?
- And your name, please?
- Sorry, how do you spell that?
- OK, thanks. It won't be long. Bye!

Partner B
- Du sagst, du möchtest etwas bestellen.
- Du bestellt einmal die Nummer 12 und zweimal die Nummer 56.
- Du verneinst und fragst, wie lange es dauern wird.
- Du anwortest, dass du in der Castle Road Nummer 134 wohnst.
- Die Nummer ist 07785 344 299.
- Du nennst deinen Nachnamen: Kreutzer.
- K-r-e-u-t-z-e-r.
- Du bedankst und verabschiedest dich.

Before role play 3, change roles. The person who was Partner A is now Partner B.

Making a doctor's appointment

3

Partner A (Read the text. You start)
- Good morning, Heartfield Medical Centre, how can I help?
- Yes, there are, do you need to see the doctor or the nurse?
- Then I can offer you an appointment at 1.30 or 3 pm.
- OK then, can I take your name, please?
- Great. See you on Wednesday, then. Bye!

Partner B
- Du fragst, ob es noch Termine für Mittwoch gibt.
- Du sagst, du hättest gerne einen Termin beim Arzt.
- Du sagst, 15 Uhr wäre perfekt.
- Du nennst deinen Namen: Nina Joachims.
- Du bedankst und verabschiedest dich.

Compare your dialogues with the examples on p. 115.

If you need some help, look at these phrases:

Language for formal phone calls
Hello, please could I speak to ...? • Speaking. • I am phoning to / because ... • Please could you tell me ... • Hold on, please. • Who's calling, please? • Please could you repeat .... • I think you have the wrong number. • Thank you for calling. • Please could you spell ... • ...

Survival English

12 What to do if you don't know a word

Imagine you are in a country where people don't understand German, and you don't have a dictionary. How can you explain what you need?

If you don't know a word, try to explain it by using relative clauses.

Excuse me, please, I'm looking for / I need to find…
- a shop where …
- a doctor who / that …
- a thing which / that …
- a machine that / where …
- a building / place where …

Hello, I'm looking for a building where …

a) Read the list of German words below. Write down what you would say if you were abroad without a dictionary and needed to find each place or thing.

Krankenhaus: **A place where doctors work, and where ill people go to get better.**

1. Apotheke: _____

2. Fundbüro: _____

3. Botschaft: _____

4. Fahrplan: _____

5. Reisezentrum: _____

Compare your answers with the answers on p.115.

b) Work with a partner. Each of you think of three places or things, and take it in turns to describe them to each other. Your partner has to guess what it is you are talking about. You can ask each other questions, too.

c) Work with a partner. Look at the cards below. Try to describe the words at the top to your partner without using any of the other words on the card. Take it in turns.

Dentist	Bank	River	School
• tooth / teeth • pain	• money • building	• water • sea	• children • learn

Survival English

13 False friends

There are a number of English words that are similar to German words, but have different meanings. This can be confusing, so it's important to recognise some of the most common ones.

a) Look at the table below. It shows some common false friends. Fill in the blank spaces. Use a dictionary.

English	German	False friend (Ger)	False friend translation
become	werden	bekommen	to get
also	auch	also	so
chef	Küchenchef	Chef	_____
_____	Öffentlichkeit	Publikum	audience
handy	_____	Handy	mobile phone
arm	Arm	_____	poor
_____	nicht dürfen	nicht müssen	not to have to / needn't

Check your answers on p. 115.

There are also some numbers that are false friends:

English	German	False friend (Ger)	False friend translation
half 8	halb 9	halb 8	half 7
billion	Milliarde	Billion	trillion

b) Find two more false friend examples and write them into the table below.

English	German	False friend (Ger)	False friend translation
_____	_____	_____	_____
_____	_____	_____	_____

111

Survival English: Solutions

1 Being polite when asking information

a) 1. Do you think you could tell me where the nearest post office is, please?
2. I wonder whether you would be able to help me with this heavy bag, please?
3. Would you be able to tell me how far it is to the Globe Theatre, please?
4. It is possible that you could change a 10 pound note for me, please?

b) *1 At the station*
A Good morning.
B Hello, how can I help (you)?
A How much is a ticket to London, please?
B It's 20 pounds.
A Thank you. Also, I didn't understand the last announcement. What was it about?
B It was telling passengers that any unattended luggage will be removed.
A Oh, I see! Thank you very much for your help. Goodbye.
B You're welcome. Goodbye!

2 At the tourist information office
A Good afternoon.
B Hello! How can I help (you)?
A I was wondering, are the shops here open on Sundays?
B Yes, most of them are, although only from 10 until 4.
A OK. Please could you tell me if there is a good club here? If so, what's it called?
B Yes, there's a good one by the main station. It's called 'Arena'.
A Fantastic! Thanks for your help. Bye!
B No problem, goodbye.

3 At the newsagent's
A Hello.
B Good afternoon.
A Can you help me, please? Can I buy a phone card here?
B Yes, we have different kinds of phone cards.
A OK, well I need to make some calls to Germany. But I'd like the cheapest card you have, please.
B Well our cheapest one is five pounds.
A Great, I'll have one of those, please. Thank you.
B Here you go. That's five pounds then. Thank you. Bye!

4 At the museum
A Hello.
B Good morning. What can I do for you?
A Could you tell me how much it costs to get in, please?
B Of course, it's 10 pounds.
A Is there a discount for young people?
B Yes, actually, there is. Young people and students get in for 5 pounds.
A Great, I'd like one ticket then, please.
B Yes, of course. Here you go. That's five pounds, please. Have a good visit!

2 Asking and explaining the way

a) A Excuse me, I'm looking for the German embassy. Do you know where it is?
B Yes, it's near the cathedral, 61 Priory Road.
A OK. How far is it?
B It's not far – only about ten minutes away on foot.
A Fantastic. Thank you very much for your help.
B You're welcome. Bye!

b) 1. Ich habe mich verlaufen.
2. Gehen Sie an der Ampel links.
3. Wie komme ich am besten nach/zum/zur …?
4. Folgen Sie den Schildern zur Stadtmitte.
5. Entschuldigen Sie bitte. Ich bin hier fremd. Könnten Sie …?

c) Individuelle Dialoge

3 Getting to know people

a) Hello, I'm Rob/Jo/…
What's your name?
So how do you know Jack/Sarah/…?
How long have you known Carl/Rose/… for?
So who do you know here?
Where do you go to school?

b) *Questions:*
What sort of a person are you?
What's your family like?
Do you have any brothers or sisters?
What's your favourite band?

Answers:
I'm open and self-confident.
It's pretty big!
I have two brothers.
Well, at the moment White Lies are definitely my favourite band – I just love them!

c) Individuelle Dialoge
d) Individuelle Lösungen; Beispiel:

Dear Brooke,
Hi, how are you? I found out today that you are my exchange partner, so I thought I would write to you and introduce myself!
My name is Lena, I'm 15 years old and I live in Aachen. Aachen is quite a small town, near Cologne. In my free time I like to go to concerts and play my flute – I guess I'm pretty musical! I also love basketball, and I play in my school team. My family is really small, I have no brothers or sisters. What about you? What do you like to do when

Survival English: Solution

you're not at school? Do you have a favourite band? And what about your family – do you have any brothers and sisters?
I have to go now – lots of homework to do!
I hope to hear from you soon.
Take care,
Lena

4 Talking about feelings

a) 1. Nice to meet you. / I'm really pleased to meet you.
2. I'm really happy / I'm so excited, what a great present!
3. I'm so relieved that nothing bad happened.
4. I feel terrible / really ill.
5. I'm so disappointed – my favourite band has stopped playing live!
6. My brother and sister are so annoying!

b) 1.
Dear Diary,
Today was such a terrible day. I'm so glad it's over. First of all I found out that I had failed my history exam. I was so embarrassed and angry at myself. I never fail exams! And then I argued with Matt. It was such a stupid argument. I was angry at him, but now I'm just sad. And lonely … Maybe I should ring him and say I'm sorry …

2.
Dear Diary,
What a great day! This morning I went shopping with Anne and found an amazing dress. I was so happy. And Anne kept saying how great I looked in it, which made me
a bit embarrassed but also really pleased. Then Mum and Dad told Dale and me that we are going to Australia this summer! I'm so excited, I've never been there. I'm a bit nervous and scared though, because of all the dangerous animals …

c) Individuelle Lösungen
d) —

5 Writing letters and e-mails

a) 1. F   2. I   3. I   4. F

b) 1. Can you tell me / let me know …
2. I'm really sorry, but I'm afraid I can't come on Tuesday.
3. Please would you be able to send me your …
4. Thanks for replying.

c) 1.
Dear Sir / Madam,
I am writing to you to ask about a poster that I ordered from you. It was supposed to be delivered to me last week, but I have not received it. My order number is 03455-56.
I wonder whether you would be able to tell me what has happened and why I haven't yet received it? Many thanks in advance.
Yours faithfully,
Robert Fields

2.
Dear Mrs Frost,
I saw on your website that you are looking for a receptionist, and am writing to you to apply for the position. I am a very organized and reliable person, and worked as a receptionist when I did my work experience last year. I really enjoyed it, which is why I am applying for this job. However, I would not be able to start until the beginning of July, because of school. Would that be a problem?
I look forward to hearing from you.
Yours sincerely,
Cara Greene

d) 1.
Hey Phil,
Thanks for your e-mail, it was great to hear from you. But I think there's been a problem with our e-mails. I wrote to you two weeks ago, but it looks like you didn't receive it. Sorry about that!
I don't have much time now but I'll write again soon!
Best wishes,
Ulli

2.
Hi Emma,
How are you? Are you excited about your trip now? This time next week you'll be here! Please would you send me your flight details? What exact time do you arrive? I can't wait to see you.
Speak to you soon.
Love,
Connor

6 Disagreeing with people

a) 1. Sorry, but I think you may have made a mistake. / Sorry, but I think my change should be $4.50, not $2.50. / Please could you check my change again?
2. No way, ManU is so much better! / I don't agree, ManU is the best club!
3. Would you mind if we went for dinner instead? / I don't feel like going to the cinema, is that OK?
4. It's important to me – my grandparents lived through World War II. / Sorry, but I think it is important that we learn about the war.
5. I did reply to your text! / How strange that you didn't get it, I definitely replied!

b) Individuelle Dialoge

Survival English: Solution

7 Buying shoes and clothes

a) Individuelle Dialoge

b)

phrases used by customers	situations in which the phrases are used
I've changed my mind.	when a customer doesn't like any of the products in a shop, e.g. after trying on different clothes or after looking at a variety of products
I'd like to exchange this/these for ...	when a customer bought something and took it home but then saw that it wasn't the right thing
Could I have my money back, please?	when a customer takes a product back to the shop but doesn't want to exchange it
I'd like to return this/these ...	when a customer takes a product back to the shop; it could also be a product which they have only tested and not yet paid for
It's too big/too small/broken	used to explain why a customer is returning something
phrases used by shop assistants	
Can I ask why you're returning it?	used when a customer returns something
Can I help you?	used to address a customer when they enter a shop

c) Individuelle Dialoge

8 Measurements and numbers

a) 1. He lives 2 miles away from his school.
2. You need 3 ounces of sugar for the recipe.
3. She weighs 10 stone.

b) 1. halb neun
2. 18. Juli
3. Viertel nach neun
4. Viertel nach drei
5. 11. September
6. 6. Januar

c) —
d) Lösungskontrolle mithilfe der CD
e) —

9 Buying and ordering food

a) Good morning, I'd like five white rolls, please.
Certainly. Is there <u>anything</u> else?
Yes. I'd also like two <u>pieces</u> of cake – what <u>kinds</u> do you have?
Well, today's <u>specials</u> are chocolate, coffee and cheesecake. Personally I'd <u>recommend</u> the cheesecake!
Then I'll have two pieces of cheesecake, please.
OK ... that <u>comes</u> to six pounds, then, please.
Great. Here <u>you go</u>. Bye!
Goodbye!

b) Individuelle Dialoge

c)

phrases used by customers	situations in which the phrases are used
Let me talk to the chef / the manager.	when the food or the service is really bad
Sorry, this isn't what I ordered!	when a customer is served the wrong food
I'm sorry, but this tastes ...	when a customer doesn't like the food or expected something completely different
I think you've made a mistake.	when a customer is served the wrong food or when there is a problem with the bill
I'd just like the bill, please.	when a customer wants to pay
phrases used by waiters / waitresses	
I'm ever so sorry.	when a waiter / waitress has made a mistake, e.g. when he / she has served the wrong food

d) phrases used by customers
Could I have an extra helping of cheese, please?
Could you perhaps reheat my meal?
Excuse me? The menu says this meal comes with a salad.
I'm sorry, I ordered lasagne without garlic, but there is really a lot of garlic in this.

phrases used by waiters / waitresses
I'm sorry your meal is not as good as you expected.
What do you think about X?
I could get you a replacement dish.
Would that be satisfactory?

10 Understanding spoken announcements

1. Der Zug, der um 15:35 Uhr nach Bristol fährt, hat wegen eines Unfalls ungefähr 25 Minuten Verspätung. Er fährt jetzt von Gleis 3 ab.
2. Passagiere des Air-Berlin-Flugs AB8112 nach Manchester können jetzt am Flugsteig / Gate 2 an Bord gehen. Die Reihen 15 bis 32 sollen als Erstes einsteigen. Man muss den Pass und die Bordkarte zeigen.
3. Es gibt Designer-T-Shirts aus Baumwolle in vier Größen zum Sonderpreis. Man kauft eines für 7,99 und bekommt ein weiteres umsonst.

4. Vorsicht an der Bahnsteigkante!
5. Eine Feuerübung findet statt. Man muss das Gebäude sofort durch den nächsten Notausgang verlassen. Man soll schnell gehen, aber nicht rennen. Die Klassen sollen sich auf dem Schulhof zusammenstellen und auf ihren Lehrer warten.
6. Wegen Bauarbeiten wird der Zug am nächsten Bahnhof enden. Ein Bus steht für die Weiterfahrt bereit. Einzelheiten kann man den Durchsagen am Bahnhof entnehmen.
7. Man soll sein Gepäck immer bei sich haben. Unbeaufsichtigtes Gepäck wird vom Sicherheitspersonal entfernt.

11 On the phone

a) 1. Hazledean Road
2. 0044 2392 995 607
3. Wilbraham
4. Massachusetts
5. 01764 334 587
6. 001 613 492 4635

b) —

c)

Formal	Informal
Good morning, please could I speak to …?	Oh, hi, is that Claire?
Would the 6th of January suit you?	Can you give me your phone number again?
Would you mind telling me your address, please?	See you later!
	What do you reckon?

d) Individuelle Dialoge

e) *1. A wrong number*
   A Hello, could I speak to Jake please?
   B Who's calling, please?
   A This is Rob Brown, I'd like to speak to Jake, please.
   B Sorry, I think you have the wrong number. My name is John, no one called Jake lives here.
   A Oh, isn't that 01647 646360?
   B Please could you repeat the number?
   A Sure, it's 01647 646360, in Okehampton.
   B That is the right number, but Jake doesn't live here!
   A Sorry, I must have the wrong number. Sorry to trouble you. Goodbye.
   B Don't worry. Goodbye.

   2. Ordering pizza
   A Good evening, Angelo's Pizzas.
   B Hello, I'd like to place an order, please.
   A OK, what would you like?
   B One number twelve, and two lots of number 56, please.
   A Right … OK, I've got that. Anything else?
   B No, thank you. How long will it be?
   A Um, it should be ready in about 20 minutes. What's your address?
   B It's 134 Castle Road.

   A And your phone number?
   B It's 07785 344 299.
   A And your name, please?
   B My surname is Kreutzer.
   A Sorry, how do you spell that?
   B K-r-e-u-t-z-e-r.
   A OK, thanks. It won't be long. Bye!
   B Thank you. Goodbye.

   3. Making a doctor's appointment
   A Good morning, Heartfield Medical Centre, how can I help?
   B Please could you tell me whether there are still appointments for Wednesday?
   A Yes, there are. Do you need to see the doctor or the nurse?
   B I'd like to see a doctor, please.
   A Then I can offer you an appointment at 1.30 or 3pm.
   B 3pm would be perfect.
   A OK then, can I take your name, please?
   B Yes, it's Nina Joachims.
   A Great. See you on Wednesday, then. Bye!
   B Thank you. Goodbye.

12 What to do if you don't know a word

a) 1. Apotheke: *A shop where you buy medicine*
2. Fundbüro: *The place you go to if you have lost something in a public place*
3. Botschaft: *The building where people work who represent their country abroad*
4. Fahrplan: *A list with the departure and arrival times of trains, buses, or planes*
5. Reisezentrum: *A place where you can get information about travelling and where you can book trips*

b) —
c) —

13 False friends

a) chef – Küchenchef – Chef – *boss*
public – Öffentlichkeit – Publikum – *audience*
handy – praktisch – Handy – *mobile phone*
arm – Arm – arm – *poor*
must not – nicht dürfen – nicht müssen – *not to have to / needn't*

b) gift – Geschenk – Gift – *poison*
sea – Meer – See – *lake*
still – immer noch – still – *quiet*
brave – mutig – brav – *good / well-behaved / honest*
director – Regisseur – Direktor – *headteacher / headmaster*
floor – Fußboden – Flur – *hall*
meaning – Bedeutung – Meinung – *opinion / view*
note – Notiz – Note – *mark / grade*

Language in Focus

1R Remember? Steigerung der Adjektive • comparison of adjectives

- Um Personen, Gegenstände oder Aktivitäten zu vergleichen, steigert man die Adjektive, die sie beschreiben.
  The runner in the middle is faster than the runner on the left.
  The runner on the right is the fastest.

- Alle einsilbigen Adjektive und die zweisilbigen Adjektive, die auf -le, -y, -er, und -ow enden, werden mit -er und -est gesteigert.
  clean – cleaner – (the) cleanest
  simple – simpler – simplest
  dirty – dirtier – dirtiest
  clever – cleverer – cleverest
  narrow – narrower – narrowest
  big – bigger – biggest

  ⚠ Beachte, dass sich manchmal die Schreibweise ändert: das stumme -e fällt weg, das -y wird zu -i, ein Konsonant nach kurzem Vokal wird verdoppelt.

- Alle anderen Adjektive werden mit more und most gesteigert.
  difficult – more difficult – most difficult
  dangerous – more dangerous – most dangerous
  It was more challenging than I thought.

- „Negative" Steigerungen werden mit less und least gebildet.
  A pony is less dangerous than a tiger.

2R Remember? Die Verlaufsform im present perfect • present perfect progressive

- Du benutzt das *present perfect progressive,* um auszudrücken, dass etwas in der Vergangenheit angefangen hat und immer noch andauert. Dabei betonst du die Handlung selbst oder die Dauer.

- Das *present perfect progressive* bildest du so:
  Form von **have** (has/have) + **been** + **-ing**-Form des Verbs

- **Bob and Mary** have been playing **chess for three hours.** (Sie spielen immer noch.)

- **Emma** has been swimming **since last summer.** (Sie hat es letzten Sommer gelernt und macht es seitdem immer wieder.)

3R Remember? Zeitangaben mit for und since • time expressions with for and since

- Wenn du sagen willst, wie lange etwas schon andauert, benutzt du eine Zeitangabe mit **for**:
  I've been playing football for three years.

  ⚠ for + Zeitraum

- Wenn du sagen willst, wann etwas begonnen hat, das noch andauert, benutzt du eine Zeitangabe mit **since**:
  I've been street BMXing since my 13th birthday.

  ⚠ since + Zeitpunkt

Language in Focus

Remember? Modalverben und ihre Ersatzformen ● modals and their substitute forms

Die Modalverben geben an, ob etwas erlaubt oder notwendig ist. Die meisten Modalverben kannst du nur im *present tense* benutzen. Ansonsten musst du Ersatzformen *(substitute forms)* benutzen.

a) **Fähigkeit**: Mit **can** und **be able to** kannst du sagen, was jemand kann.

	PRESENT TENSE	PAST TENSE	PRESENT PERFECT	FUTURE
MODALVERB	can	could	–	–
	can't	couldn't	–	–
ERSATZFORM	be able to	was/were able to	has/have been able to	will be able to
	not be able to	wasn't/weren't able to	hasn't/haven't been able to	won't/will not be able to

When Lily was four she could already read. When Lily was four she was already able to read.
● **Could** benutzt du auch für höfliche Bitten: **Could** someone open the window, please?

b) **Erlaubnis**: **Can, mustn't** und **(not) be allowed to** benutzt du, wenn du um etwas bittest, um Erlaubnis fragst oder jemandem etwas erlaubst oder verbietest.

	PRESENT TENSE	PAST TENSE	PRESENT PERFECT	FUTURE
MODALVERB	can	could	–	–
	can't	couldn't	–	–
	mustn't	–	–	–
ERSATZFORM	be allowed to	was/were allowed to	has/have been allowed to	will be allowed to
	not be allowed to	wasn't/weren't allowed to	hasn't/haven't been allowed to	won't/will not be allowed to

You can swim in the pool but you aren't allowed to swim in the lake. You mustn't swim in the sea either.

c) **Notwendigkeit**: Du benutzt **must** oder **has to/have to**, um zu sagen, was jemand tun muss. Wenn du sagen willst, dass jemand etwas nicht tun muss, d. h. nicht zu tun braucht, benutzt du **doesn't have to/don't have to** oder **needn't**.

	PRESENT TENSE	PAST TENSE	PRESENT PERFECT	FUTURE
MODALVERB	must	–	–	–
	needn't/ doesn't/don't need to	–	–	–
ERSATZFORM	has/have to	had to	has/have had to	will have to
	doesn't/don't have to	didn't have to	hasn't/haven't had to	won't/will not have to

Language in Focus

> You **must** tidy up your room. You **have to** tidy up your room.
> I **had to** go to the post office yesterday.
> You **don't need to/needn't** do your homework now.
> You **don't have to** finish your meal if you are full.

> d) Empfehlung: Mit **should (not)** drückst du aus, dass etwas deiner Meinung nach (nicht) so sein sollte oder erfragst die Meinung einer anderen Person.
> Hier gibt es nur die Formen **should / shouldn't** bzw. **should have / shouldn't have**.
> You **should** be in a good physical condition to play a sport.
> You **shouldn't have** eaten that much chocolate.

Remember? Das Passiv ● the passive

> - Wenn mit einer Person, einem Tier oder einer Sache etwas getan wird, kannst du das durch das Passiv ausdrücken. Man benutzt es dann, wenn nicht wichtig oder nicht klar ist, wer handelt oder gehandelt hat.
>
>   Das Passiv in der Gegenwart bildest du so: Gegenwarts-Form von **be** (am/is/are) + *past participle*
>   Thousands of animals **are kept** in filthy sheds.
>   Das Passiv in der Vergangenheit bildest du so: Vergangenheits-Form von **be** (was/were) + *past participle*
>   Factory farming **was invented** in the USA.
>   The chickens **were kept** in small cages.
>   Das Passiv in der Zukunft bildest du so: Zukunfts-Form von **be** (will be) + *past participle*
>   Tomorrow the animals **will be taken** to the slaughterhouse. 
>
> *I keep my chickens in a big cage!*
>
> *We are kept in a big cage!*
>
> - Wenn du in einem Passiv-Satz die handelnde Person oder die Ursache für etwas nennen willst, musst du sie mit **by** an den Satz anhängen.
>   The more meat the animals produce, the more money **is made** (**by** the farmer).
>   Most factory farms **are run by** giant firms.

Either – or / neither – nor

Das deutsche „entweder … oder …" wird im Englischen mit "**either … or …**" ausgedrückt.
Chickens should be kept either outside or at least in bigger cages.

Wenn man im Deutschen „weder … noch …" sagt, benutzt man im Englischen "**neither … nor …**".
The animals will neither have a family nor do anything that is natural to them.

Remember? Indirekte Rede ● reported speech

- Wenn du berichten willst, was jemand sagt, benutzt du die Form der indirekten Rede. Die indirekte Rede besteht aus einem Begleitsatz und der wiedergegebenen Aussage. Beide Satzteile können durch **that** verbunden werden. Wenn die Originalaussage Wörter enthält, die nur aus dem Zu-sammenhang richtig zu verstehen sind, musst du sie in der wiedergegebenen Aussage anpassen: "I love staying in touch with my mates."
Gavin says that **he** loves staying in touch with **his** mates.

- Wenn du eine Frage wiedergeben willst, benutzt du **if** oder **whether**:
 "Does Shannon help out on the farm?"
I would like to know whether Shannon help**s** out on the farm.

- Wenn die Frage mit einem Fragewort eingeleitet wird, übernimmst du das Fragewort:
"How old are you?"
I would like to know how old she is.

Remember? Die Vorvergangenheit ● past perfect

- Wenn eine Handlung vor einer anderen Handlung in der Vergangenheit stattgefunden hat und beide Handlungen abgeschlossen sind, drückst du das mit dem *past perfect* und dem *simple past* aus. Die Handlung, die vor der anderen stattgefunden hat, steht im *past perfect*. Das *past perfect* bildest du so: **had** + *past participle*
I did my work experience in a flower shop – I had sent them my CV two months before.

Remember? Zeitverschiebung in indirekter Rede ● tense shift in reported speech

- Wenn du berichten willst, was jemand gesagt hat, benutzt du die indirekte Rede. Das Verb im Begleitsatz steht dabei in der Vergangenheit *(said, told, asked)*. Die Zeitform der wiedergegebenen Rede rückt dann sozusagen eine Stufe weiter zurück in die Vergangenheit. Diesen Vorgang nennt man Zeitverschiebung.

"It's a big salon." PRESENT	Nadira said (that)	it was a big salon. PAST
"I was a bit worried." PAST	Nadira said (that)	she had been a bit worried. PAST PERFECT
"My work experience week has been a valuable experience for me." PRESENT PERFECT	Nadira said (that)	her work experience week had been a valuable experience for her. PAST PERFECT

- "will" wird zu "would"

"I will apply for an apprenticeship when I'm older."	She said (that)	she would apply for an apprenticeship when she were older.

Language in Focus

> ⚠️ In einigen Fällen ist es nicht nötig, eine Zeitform zu verschieben, z. B. wenn die Aussage immer noch gültig ist.
> Nadira: "I realized I **had** a hair dye allergy."
> **Nadira said** that she **had realized** she **had** a hair dye allergy.
> Da Nadira die Allergie zu diesem Zeitpunkt immer noch hat, bleibt die Aussage in der ursprünglichen Zeitform stehen.

Zeitangaben müssen in der indirekten Rede entsprechend angepasst werden:

today	→	that day	two months ago	→	two months earlier
last week	→	the week before	yesterday	→	the day before

LiF 10R Remember? Bedingungssätze 1 ● conditional clauses 1

Wenn du sagen willst, was unter bestimmten Bedingungen geschehen wird oder geschehen kann, benutzt du einen Bedingungssatz.
Im **if-Satz** *(if-clause)* benutzt du ein Verb im *simple present*.
Im Hauptsatz *(main clause)* benutzt du das *will future* oder ein Hilfsverb (z. B. **will, can, must, should**) mit einem Vollverb.

IF-CLAUSE	MAIN CLAUSE
If you **get** the job as a computer salesperson,	you **will work** in a team.
If you **get** the job as a computer salesperson,	you **must know** about computers.
If you **get** the job as a laboratory technician,	you **can work** independently.

LiF 11 Indirekte Fragen mit Zeitverschiebung ● reported questions with tense shift

Wenn du eine Frage wiedergeben willst, die jemand anderes in der Vergangenheit gestellt hat, benutzt du **if** oder **whether** und beachtest die Regeln für die Zeitverschiebung (LiF 9R).

"**Do** you **like** water?"	Mr Daly asked Sarosh if he **liked** water.
PRESENT	PAST
"What time **did** you **arrive** last night?"	She asked me what time I **had arrived** the night before.
PAST	PAST PERFECT
"**Have** you **seen** my exercise book?"	She asked us whether we **had seen** her exercise book.
PRESENT PERFECT	PAST PERFECT

- "will" wird zu "would"

Will I ever **get** home again?

When Robinson Crusoe was on the island he wondered whether he **would** ever **get** home again.

Language in Focus

Remember? Relativsätze ● relative clauses

- Relativsätze sind Nebensätze, die Personen oder Dinge näher beschreiben. Sie beginnen meist mit den Relativpronomen **who**, **which** oder **that**. **Who** steht für Personen, **which** für Dinge. Es gibt zwei Arten: „bestimmende Relativsätze" (*"defining relative clauses"*) und „nicht-bestimmende Relativsätze" (*"non-defining relative clauses"*).

- Bestimmende Relativsätze kann man nicht weglassen. Hier werden keine Kommas gesetzt und man kann statt **who** oder **which** auch **that** für Personen und Dinge benutzen.
  The "Wacken Open Air" is a festival that takes place every year in northern Germany.

- Nichtbestimmende Relativsätze geben Zusatzinformationen, die man nicht unbedingt braucht, um die Hauptinformation zu verstehen. Sie werden durch Kommas vom Hauptsatz getrennt.
  The popularity of "Wacken Open Air", which is one of the leading heavy metal festivals, proves that heavy metal is still going strong.

Remember? Relativsätze ● relative clauses

- Das *simple present* benutzt du, wenn du über Gewohnheiten, Tatsachen und regelmäßig vorkommende Ereignisse sprichst.
  We usually wear tight jeans and T-shirts with the names of our favourite rock bands.

- Die Verneinung von Vollverben und Fragen bildest du mit **don't**, bei *he, she, it* mit **doesn't**:
I don't like punk music.	**She doesn't** write poems.	
Do you like punk music?	Yes, I **do**.	No, I **don't**.
Does Tom play rugby?	Yes, he **does**.	No, he **doesn't**.
Is Simon a heavy metal fan?	Yes, he **is**.	No, he **isn't**.

- Das *simple present* benutzt du auch, wenn du über einen festgelegten Zeitplan (zum Beispiel Fahrpläne von Zügen oder Bussen) sprichst, der in der Zukunft liegt.
  The train leaves at 9 pm.   **The festival starts next Friday.**

Language in Focus

Remember? Die Verlaufsform der Gegenwart ● present progressive

- Das *present progressive* beschreibt Ereignisse und Handlungen, die gerade stattfinden.
  Das *present progressive* bildest du so:
  Form von **be** (am/is/are) + Verb + **ing**
  **My favourite colour is black, that's why
  I'm wearing black jeans at the moment.**

- Du verneinst die Form von **be**.
  The sun isn't shining.
  They aren't skateboarding.

  They are enjoying their meal.

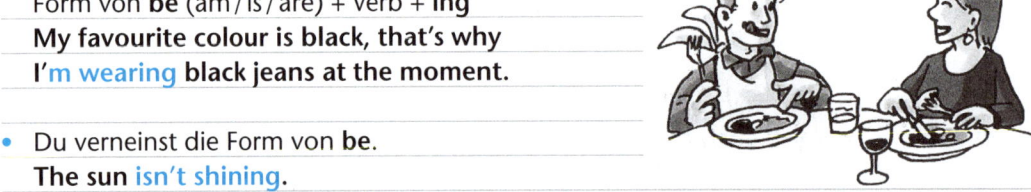

- Ja/Nein-Fragen:

Frage	bejahende Antwort	verneinende Antwort
Is she wearing black jeans at the moment?	**Yes, she is.**	**No, she isn't.**

- Fragen mit Fragewort:
  What is Joanna doing at the moment?   **Why are you leaving?**
  Where are you going?   **When is Nadira coming home?**

- Das *present progressive* benutzt du auch, wenn du über vereinbarte Pläne oder Verabredungen sprichst, die in der Zukunft liegen.
  I'm meeting Tom at nine o'clock.   **What are you doing on Saturday?**

- Diese Übersicht hilft dir zu entscheiden, wann du die einfache Form der Gegenwart und wann du die Verlaufsform benutzt:

Man verwendet das *present simple*, wenn man	Man verwendet das *present progressive*, wenn man
• über Tatsachen spricht. **The light from the sun takes a couple of minutes to reach the Earth.**	• ausdrücken möchte, was man gerade macht oder was in diesem Moment passiert. **I am sitting in the garden and reading a book.**
• über Gewohnheiten spricht. **I usually wear jeans.**	• ein Foto oder Bild beschreibt. **In that picture a man is sitting in a car.**
• über regelmäßige Ereignisse spricht. **Tourists usually take photos of the Statue of Liberty.**	
Signalwörter für das *present simple*: always, usually, often, sometimes, never, every morning/month/year, on Mondays	Signalwörter für das *present progressive*: at the moment, now

15R Remember? Die einfache Vergangenheit ● simple past

- Für Ereignisse und Handlungen, die in der Vergangenheit liegen und abgeschlossen sind, verwendest du das *simple past*. Signalwörter: **yesterday, last week, two days ago in 1950,** …
In the year 1644 the Dutch explorer Abel Tasman found out that Australia was an island.

- Das *simple past* von regelmäßigen Verben bildest du, indem du **-ed** an den Infinitiv anhängst. Bei unregelmäßigen Verben gibt es keine Regel. Du musst sie auswendig lernen. Hinten im Buch findest du eine Liste mit unregelmäßigen Verben.

- Die Verneinung bildest du bei den meisten Verben mit **didn't**, bei **was/were** mit **not**:
Michael didn't read comics anymore.
Jill and Judy weren't very happy to see us last Tuesday.

- Ja-/Nein-Fragen:

Frage	bejahende Antwort	verneinende Antwort
Did you go to the concert last night?	Yes, I did.	No, I didn't.
Was it a good film?	Yes, it was.	No, it wasn't.

- Fragen mit Fragewort: Where did you go yesterday? Why didn't you ask me to come to the party?

16R Remember? Stellung der Satzglieder ● word order

- Das Grundmuster für einfache englische Sätze ist strikt und klar:

0	1	2	3
	SUBJEKT	PRÄDIKAT	OBJEKT und andere Satzergänzungen
	Many settlers	started	sheep farms.

- Adverbien oder Konjunktionen stehen vor dem Kernsatz.

But	most of them	did not manage	to make enough money.
Finally	Aborigines	were given	full citizens' rights.

- Dieser Bauplan bleibt auch in Fragesätzen bestehen:

0	1	2	3
FRAGEWORT und ggf. Hilfsverb	SUBJEKT	PRÄDIKAT	OBJEKT und andere Satzergänzungen
Who		is	Kevin Rudd?
Why did	he	say	sorry?
Did	most of them	manage	to make enough money?
Could	the settlers	become	rich?

123

Language in Focus

- Zeit- und Ortsangaben stehen immer außerhalb des Kernsatzes. Wenn sie zusammen in einem Satz vorkommen, lautet die Regel „Ort vor Zeit". Eine Zeitangabe kann aber auch vor dem Kernsatz stehen:

ZEITANGABE	KERNSATZ	ORTSANGABE	ZEITANGABE
	Willem Janszoon sailed	into Australian waters	at the beginning of the 17th century.
At the beginning of the 17th century	Willem Janszoon sailed	into Australian waters.	

17R Remember? Die -ing-Form als Nomen ● -ing-nouns

- Wenn du im Deutschen ein Verb zu einem Nomen umformen willst, brauchst du einfach nur den Infinitiv groß zu schreiben. Im Englischen benutzt man die **-ing**-Form des Verbs:
  walking (das) Gehen   **jumping** (das) Springen

- Die **-ing**-Form als Nomen kann im Satz dieselben Aufgaben übernehmen wie jedes andere Nomen. Sie kann als Subjekt stehen:
  Raising **cattle is our business.**   Maintaining **radio contact is vital.**

- Die **-ing**-Form kann auch als Objekt im Satz stehen:
  I like living here.
- Andere Verben, hinter denen in der Regel die **-ing**-Form eines Verbs steht, sind z. B: hate, love, avoid, stop, enjoy.

18R Die -ing-Form nach Präpositionen ● -ing-nouns after prepositions

Ein **-ing**-noun steht oft nach Präpositionen.
Nomen + Präposition + **-ing**-Form:
He has a good chance of winning the race.
Verb + Präposition + **-ing**-Form:
I dream of travelling to Australia.
Adjektiv + Präposition + **-ing**-Form:
She's interested in learning Spanish.
Andere Ausdrücke, hinter denen in der Regel die **-ing**-Form als Nomen steht, sind z. B.: be good at, be bad at, look forward to, be happy about, keep on

I dream of travelling to Australia.

124

Language in Focus

19R Remember? Kurzantworten ● short answers

- Auf Ja / Nein-Fragen antwortet man normalerweise mit Kurzantworten.

SIMPLE PRESENT	bejahende Antwort	verneinende Antwort
Does John work for a non-English-speaking newspaper?	Yes, he **does**.	No, he **doesn't**.
Is Christmas in spring in Australia?	Yes, it **is**.	No, it **isn't**.
SIMPLE PAST		
Did Cathy Freeman carry the olympic torch?	Yes, she **did**.	No, she **didn't**.
Was Katie born in Australia?	Yes, she **was**.	No, she **wasn't**.

20 Present perfect mit ever ● present perfect with ever

- Wenn du fragen willst, ob jemand etwas jemals in seinem Leben gemacht hat, fängst du an mit:
  Have you ever …?
  "Have you **ever** argued with your parents about using the Internet?"

21R Remember? Bedingungssätze 2 ● conditional clauses 2

- Ein Bedingungssatz der zweiten Form drückt aus, was unter bestimmten Bedingungen geschehen könnte. Es ist möglich, aber eher unwahrscheinlich, dass diese Bedingung eintritt.
  IF-CLAUSE (NEBENSATZ MIT **if**):   MAIN CLAUSE (HAUPTSATZ):
  if + *simple past*   **would** / **could** / **might** + *infinitive*
  If I **received** insulting messages online,   I **wouldn't** reply.

22R Remember? Imperativ (Befehlsform) ● imperative

- Der Imperativ ist immer identisch mit dem Infinitiv:
  Read the privacy policies on websites.

- Die negative Form wird immer mit **do not** oder **don't** gebildet:
  Don't insult others.

- Wenn man etwas besonders betonen möchte, kann man **do** und den Infinitiv des Verbs benutzen:
  Do tell your parents if you planned to meet an online friend in real life.

125

Language in Focus

23 used to

- Den Ausdruck **used to** benutzt du, um regelmäßige Ereignisse und Gewohnheiten in der Vergangenheit zu beschreiben.
  Jodie's mother used to be a teacher when Jodie was a child.
  (Jodie's mother doesn't work as a teacher now.)

  Die Verneinung lautet **didn't use to**:
  Jodie didn't use to go to a regular school. She attended the School of the Air.

  Die Frageform lautet **Did … use to …?**
  Did Jodie use to see her classmates every day?

24R Remember? Die Verlaufsform der Vergangenheit ● past progressive

- Das past progressive drückt aus, dass eine Handlung in der Vergangenheit über einen längeren Zeitraum im Gange war: I was working in the hospital.

- Wenn zwei Ereignisse in der Vergangenheit gleichzeitig ablaufen, dann bildet das länger andauernde den „Hintergrund" für das kürzere, das sich im „Vordergrund" abspielt.
  Wir können im Deutschen zum Beispiel sagen: „Ich war gerade dabei, zu kochen", im Englischen drückt man das mit dem **past progressive** aus.
  Vordergrund-Geschehen: When Carrie arrived at the building
  Hintergrund-Geschehen: Nick was waiting there.

- Die Formen des past progressive werden ähnlich gebildet wie die Formen des present progressive. Nur steht **be** natürlich in der entsprechenden Vergangenheitsform:

FORMEL	was / were + *(verb)*+ing
(+)	You were working in the hospital.
(−)	I wasn't working in the hospital.
(y/n)?	Were you working in the hospital?
(wh-)?	What were you doing?

  While the woman was taking a picture, a man stole her bag.

25R Remember? Verben mit zwei Objekten ● verbs with two objects

- Es gibt viele Verben, die zwei Objekte haben können. Man unterscheidet **direkte** und **indirekte** Objekte. Das indirekte Objekt steht entweder vor dem direkten Objekt oder es folgt ihm unmittelbar. Wenn das indirekte Objekt hinter dem direkten steht, dann muss es durch *to* oder *for* eingeleitet werden.
  I gave him the letter.   I gave the letter to him.

Question – answer – relationship QAR

Right there

I can find the answer in the text. The answer is in one word or one sentence. I can point at it and then write it down.

Think & search

The answer is in the text, but not in one place. I must look at different text passages for information and put it together. When I write down the answer, I must use my own words.

Text and me

I can find part of the answer in the text, but I must also add what I already know about the topic.

On my own

I can find the answer using my background knowledge and experience. I must use my own ideas and give my opinion.

Text- und Bildquellen

Textquellen: 13 adapted from: http://www.meatlessmonday.com/; 18 abridged and adapted from: http://www.workuk.co.uk/

Bildquellen: 3 (Ballon): creative collection Verlag GmbH, Freiburg; 3 (Floß): Outdoor Archiv, Hamburg; 3 (Hundeschlitten): Getty Images, München (Peter Lilja); 3 (bungee): Shutterstock Images LCC, New York, NY 10004; 5: fotolia.com , New York; 8: tree2tree GmbH, Oberhausen; 9: Shutterstock Images LCC, New York, NY 10004; 11: Cartoon Stock Ltd, Bath; 14: StockFood GmbH , München (FoodPhotogr. Eising); 16: iStockphoto, Calgary; 21: OP-online/Pressehaus Bintz-Verlag GmbH, Offenbach (Christian Endecott); 29: alamy images, Abingdon/Oxfordshire; 33 (White Lies): Picture Press Bild- und Textagentur GmbH , Hamburg; 35 (A): Getty Images, München (Jupiterimages / © PYMCA); 35 (B): alamy images, Abingdon/Oxfordshire (David Hancock); 35 (C): iStockphoto, Calgary; 36: Doomtree Records; 37: Brown, Tasmin, Surry Hills NSW; 39 (1): iStockphoto, Calgary; 39 (2): alamy images, Abingdon/Oxfordshire (Ace Stock limited); 39 (3): fotolia.com , New York; 39 (4): iStockphoto, Calgary; 39 (5): fotolia.com , New York; 39 (6): iStockphoto, Calgary; 39 (7): iStockphoto, Calgary; 39 (8): iStockphoto, Calgary; 42: Caro Fotoagentur GmbH, Berlin; 46 (Fallschirm): vario images GmbH & Co. KG, Bonn; 46 (Rafting): Deuter, Wolfgang, Germering; 46 (paragleiten): bildmaschine.de, Berlin; 46 (schnorcheln): Sea Tops, Karlsruhe; 46 (skydiving): bildagentur-online GmbH, Burgkunstadt; 46 (tauchen): alimdi.net, Deisenhofen; 53 (Volleyball): Kuttig, Siegfried , Lüneburg; 53 (Wasserski): Outdoor Archiv, Hamburg; 59 (Korallen): Sea Tops, Karlsruhe (Mark Conlin); 59 (Känguru): fotolia.com , New York; 59 (Wüste): Rieke, Michael, Hannover; 62: ullstein bild, Berlin; 65 (Brücke): Corbis, Düsseldorf (Souders); 65 (Koala): Wittmann, Antje, Straubing; 65 (Schild): iStockphoto, Calgary (Lance Bellers); 65 (skyline): fotolia.com , New York; 66 (Karte): wikimedia.commons; 68: OKAPIA KG Michael Grzimek & Co., Frankfurt am Main (Perkins/still pictures); 70: alamy images, Abingdon/Oxfordshire (Bill Bachman); 71 (unten): ullstein bild, Berlin (Imagebroker.net); 73 (E-Voting): Picture-Alliance GmbH, Frankfurt am Main (Keytone); 73 (Internetcafé): Pawlowski, Berlin; 75: fotolia.com , New York (Klaus Epple); 76: Verlag Carl Ueberreuter Ges.m.b.H., Wien; 79: fotolia.com , New York (Andres Rodriguez); 81: ullstein bild, Berlin; 84 (Helm): alamy images, Abingdon/Oxfordshire (Doug Steley); 84 (Ostermarsch): ullstein bild, Berlin (AP); 84 (Unterricht): photothek.net GbR, Radevormwald (Ute Grabowsky); 85: Picture-Alliance GmbH, Frankfurt am Main (United Archivs); 87: alamy images, Abingdon/Oxfordshire (Caro); 92 (Jugendliche): fotolia.com , New York; 92 (Logo): Picture-Alliance GmbH, Frankfurt am Main (Stache); 92 (Mutter und Kind): iStockphoto, Calgary; 92 (Wasser): fotolia.com , New York; 93: ullstein bild, Berlin (Granger Collection); 94 (Demonstration): imagetrust, Koblenz (Manfred Vollmer); 94 (Skulptur): ullstein bild, Berlin (united archives).